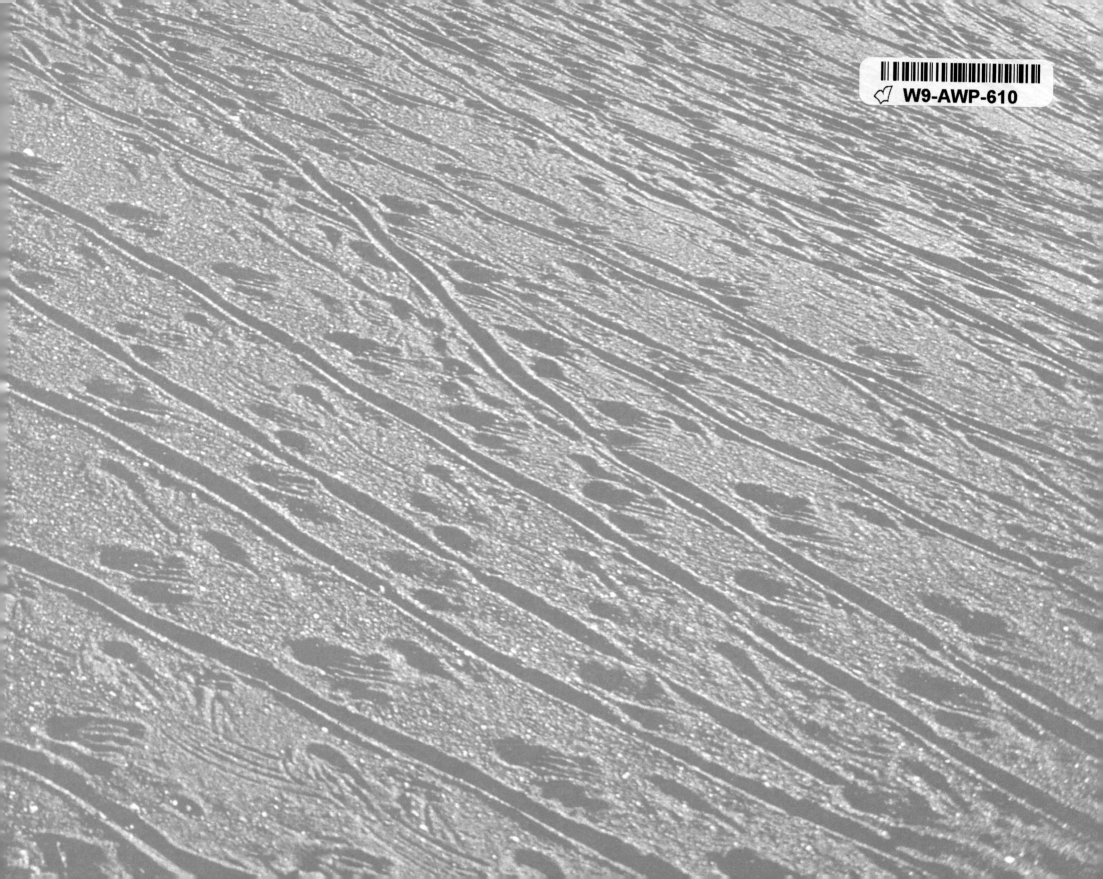

GALAPAGOS
Islands Born of Fire

10th Anniversary Edition

GALAPAGOS
Islands Born of Fire

TUI DE ROY

Princeton University Press
Princeton and Oxford

Opening photographs:
Front cover: *Marine iguana with lava flow entering the sea, Cape Hammond, Fernandina.*
Back cover & page 1: *Magnificent frigate male carrying nesting material, Seymour.*
Endpapers: *Marine iguana tracks, Cape Douglas, Fernandina.*
Page 2: *A river of molten lava illuminates a palo santo forest on its way to the sea, Fernandina, February 1995.*
Page 3: *Overwhelmed by heat from steaming lava, marine iguanas attempt to cool down by sky pointing, Cape Hammond, Fernandina.*
Page 4: *A female land iguana pauses at the caldera edge before descending within to nest, Fernandina.*
Page 5: *Giant tortoises mating on the caldera floor during the rainy season, Alcedo Volcano, Isabela.*
Page 6: *Green turtles and yellowtail surgeonfish share lush algae pastures bathed by upwellings, Cape Douglas, Fernandina.*
Page 7: *A nocturnal swallow-tailed gull rests near a roaring blowhole, Punta Suarez, Española.*
Page 8: *Peaceful neighbours, flamingos share their salt lagoon with a resting sea lion, Rabida.*
Page 9: *A flock of courting flamingos reels in unison over arid hills, Punta Cormorant, Floreana.*
Page 10: *A giant tortoise wanders the caldera rim of Alcedo Volcano in the dry season, Isabela.*
Page 11: *A playful bottlenose dolphin leaps into the morning sun, Punta Vicente Roca, Isabela.*
Title page: *Cape Douglas sunrise, Fernandina.*
Page 16: *Lava fountains and spatter cone formation flank vents on Cerro Azul, Isabela.*

First published in 1998 by David Bateman Ltd, 30 Tarndale Grove,
Albany, Auckland, New Zealand
Reprinted 1999, 2004
Tenth Anniversary Edition first published in 2007

Published in the United States and Canada in 2010 by Princeton University Press,
41 William Street, Princeton, New Jersey 08540

ISBN 978-0-691-14637-9
Library of Congress Control Number: 2009935113

press.princeton.edu

Cover design by Shelley Watson
Design by Chris O'Brien/Pages Literary Pursuits
Printed in China through Colorcraft Ltd., Hong Kong

5 7 9 10 8 6

To Mark

whose constant companionship and shared vision of nature
has transformed life into an endless journey of discovery.

CONTENTS

Acknowledgements

When writing a book that touches upon your entire life's career, plus memories going back to earliest childhood, how could one ever thank all those who made it possible? There were family, friends and neighbours who shared meaningful moments of ordinary life; visiting scientists, film-makers, writers and explorers who shared their knowledge and enthusiasm; the many hard-working conservationists who laboured selflessly to preserve our precious islands; and mentors far away who coaxed my photographic passion into a fulfilling profession.

My parents who nurtured and taught me, my brother who shared all of my childhood dreams and discoveries, and a thousand other people who each in their own way contributed to making me who I am are remembered and thanked. A few names stand out in particular, even though for each one mentioned there are dozens of others equally important. When I was fifteen Jack Couffer, a Disney film-maker, gave me a quality camera which produced my first published photographs. George Lindsay, director of the California Academy of Sciences, imbued in me enough confidence as a teenager to write my first articles and deliver lectures to large audiences. At the same time Julian Fitter, friend and neighbour, entrusted me with the leadership of his passengers in the early days of Galapagos tourism and in so doing enabled me to fly from the nest. David Cavagnaro, entomologist, naturalist, writer and photographer, inspired and encouraged me to write my first book. Les Line, as editor of *Audubon* magazine, took me under his wing and propelled me into the exciting world of freelance nature photography, whereas his photo editor Ann Guilfoyle gave me an inside view through her friendship and advice. Likewise Barbara Burn, editor of my first book, became a long-time friend. For more than twenty years, Jonathan Fisher, editor of *International Wildlife* magazine has patiently guided my writings through two score articles, while Karen Altpeter, Steve Freligh and John Nuhn whittled photo layouts from the mountains of images submitted.

Tom Simkin, and his many vulcanologist colleagues, allowed me to join their field trips into the bowels of active Galapagos volcanoes and imparted their love and understanding of these wildest of places. My first husband Alan Moore shared my adventures and taught me about the practical side of conservation. Miguel Cifuentes, who through his determination built the National Park's unshakable foundations, inspired me to believe in a better conservation future. I have admired Linda Cayot over the years for her dogged energy and expertise in defence of our endangered reptiles.

In recent times, Eliecer Cruz, dedicating his life to Galapagos as the first native born National Park Director, has renewed my belief that these islands can indeed be saved, along with Rob Bensted-Smith, first as dear friend and later as Darwin Station Director. Sven-Olof Lindblad's vision for revitalizing support for the future through the tourism industry raised these hopes to unprecedented heights.

For many years underwater photographer and author Paul Humann provided a vital lifeline with the real world of cameras and film in the absence of a reliable postal service, carrying by hand more gear on international flights than I'm sure he'd care to remember. Godfrey Merlen, independent thinker and tireless conservationist; Jack Grove, Galapagos enthusiast and researcher; David Day, ever adventuresome naturalist and activist; Lynn Fowler, 'sister' and confidante, are but a few of the friends who have enriched my Galapagos experiences.

For their personal touch and professional contributions I wish to thank all the personnel of the Galapagos National Park and Darwin Research Station, as well as the ship's captains, crew and guides, past and present, with whom I've spent time in these wonderful islands.

Finally, Colin and Betty Monteath, together with Denali and Carys, have provided endless support and friendship, making our new life in New Zealand possible. Colin's firm nudgings are responsible for the birth of this book. My thanks to Tracey Borgfeldt and her team at David Bateman Limited for support and understanding during its production, especially Chris O'Brien who carefully united text and photos. And to Mark for his constant and invaluable input and for patiently compiling the index.

Most of all, I thank Mark for sharing this view of life as one, for his closeness and for his caring nature, and for simply being who he is.

Foreword

The environmental problems faced by Galapagos today are many, marring these islands' world conservation status and threatening their biodiversity even as these fundamental elements remain key to all development efforts.

As has been repeated countless times, the oceanic character and geographic isolation of Galapagos has blessed these islands with a unique flora and fauna that evolved to adapt to an inhospitable environment. At the same time, this situation has produced an ecosystem that is highly vulnerable to outside factors such as the arrival of man and his retinue of introduced species. From the biologist's perspective, the marine environment, conditioned by converging oceanic currents, is every bit as extraordinary as, or perhaps even more so than, its terrestrial counterpart.

The pressures that have come to bear on these remarkable environments are fundamentally man-made, their repercussions potentially irreversible. The costs of fighting or controlling these threats are indeed exceptionally high, the test of the future lying in balancing these factors so that the human presence ceases to act as an extraneous burden. The human presence needs to become linked to the natural systems and their ecological limiters, and be converted into a contributing force toward the archipelago's restoration and recovery from past impact, thus becoming a model to be emulated in other parts of the world. In every way possible economic development should be nature-based, in such a way as to demonstrate that man need not act as an alien influence, but rather can become an integral part of the biodiversity whole, respecting and sharing the environment with its native species. This is the true challenge for the government of Ecuador as the custodian of this double World Heritage Site.

Currently Galapagos is undergoing an array of negative processes that need to be evaluated in a holistic manner. Future actions must be focused on management priorities that guarantee conservation of complete ecosystems, including the connectivity of their biological and evolutionary functions. Only this approach will allow the full ecological health of Galapagos to be maintained, thereby ensuring the continued generation of natural goods and services for the benefit of the local inhabitants.

There is no doubt that the future of both Galapagos and Galapagueños is under threat. An analysis of the current problems can be summarised as follows: Introduced species settling down and competing with native and endemic ones; fast accelerating human population growth curve, passing 18,000 in 2001 and reaching around 27,000 today, and still growing; energy dependence on mainland fuel supplies, with attendant risk of oil spills far greater than those already experienced; mainland food supply dependency, with danger of increasing accidental pest species introductions; weakening of the principal conservation institutions, allowing for chaotic economic growth and severe indications of corruption; drop in agricultural production, with farmland being abandoned and converting to breeding grounds for exotic plant pests; illegal fishing activities centred on shark finning and dwindling sea cucumbers for Asian markets, creating false expectations among local fishermen and damaging the marine ecosystem; and mushrooming, disorganized tourism development.

Even if we think of the future in purely economic terms, should the above tendencies not be corrected in time, the very losers will be ourselves, the island inhabitants. Forgetting our ethical and moral responsibilities to preserve this living laboratory of evolution for the entire world disregards the fact that our future wellbeing rests directly on the health of the island ecosystem.

Rethinking our management model of this fantastic archipelago is therefore paramount and urgent. There is still time, but we must all show our willingness to move together in that direction: The government, the local people, regional authorities, the fishing community, tourism enterprises, to name but a few. We must draw the course of development guided by the limitations of the ecosystem itself. Should the human species in Galapagos fail to establish a blueprint for true sustainable development, where else in the world will this be possible?

Eliecer Cruz, Santa Cruz, April 2007

Eliecer Cruz is a native Galapagueño born on Floreana Island, with a master's degree in biology. From 1996 to 2003 he was Director of the Galapagos National Park, and is now the Ecuador representative for the World Wildlife Fund for Nature (WWF).

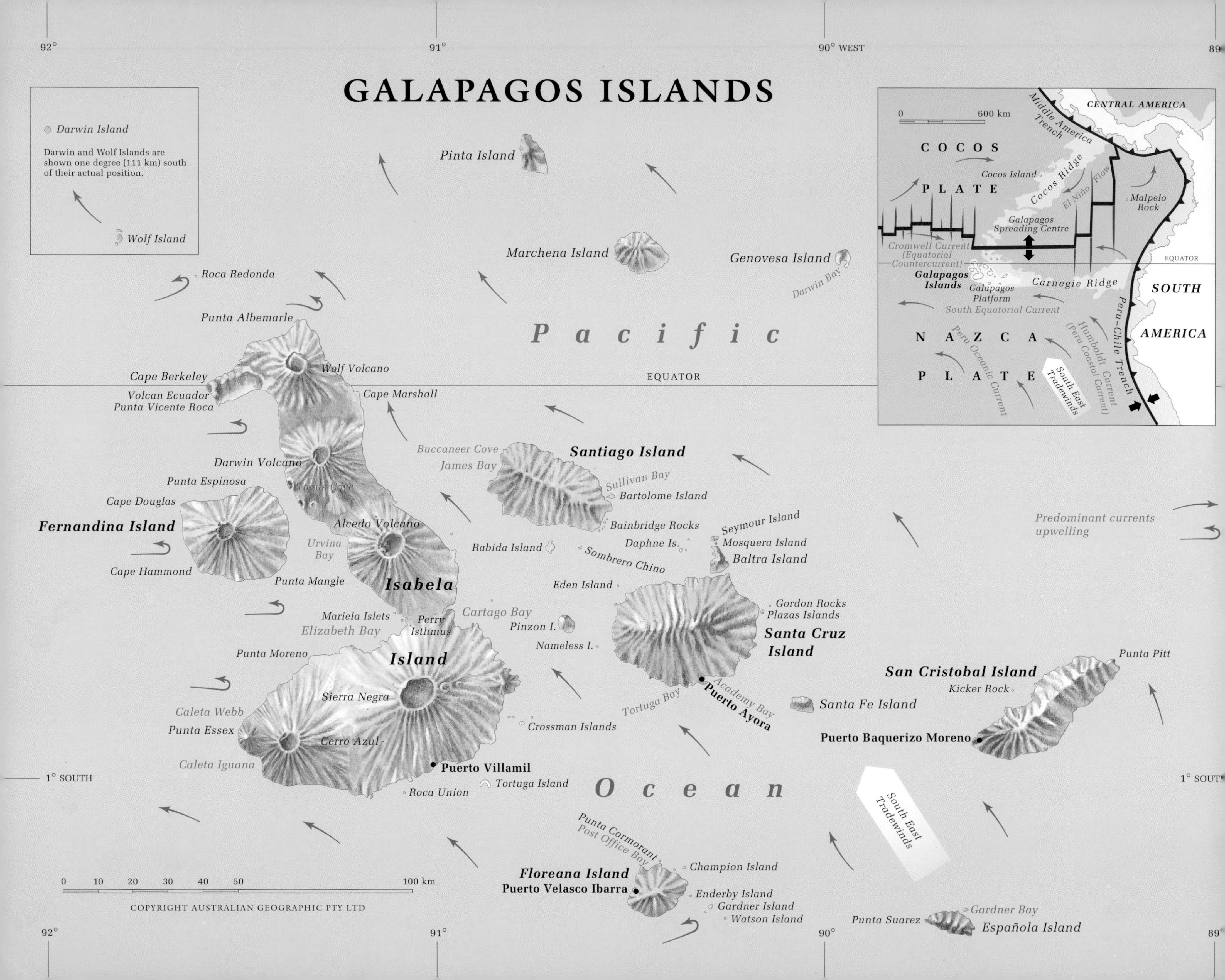

GALAPAGOS ISLANDS

Darwin Island

Darwin and Wolf Islands are shown one degree (111 km) south of their actual position.

Wolf Island

Pinta Island

Marchena Island

Genovesa Island

Darwin Bay

Roca Redonda

Punta Albemarle

Pacific

Cape Berkeley

Wolf Volcano

EQUATOR

Volcan Ecuador
Punta Vicente Roca

Cape Marshall

Buccaneer Cove

Santiago Island

Darwin Volcano

James Bay

Punta Espinosa

Tagus Cove

Sullivan Bay

Bartolome Island

Cape Douglas

Fernandina Island

Alcedo Volcano

Bainbridge Rocks

Seymour Island

Urvina Bay

Daphne Is.

Mosquera Island

Rabida Island

Baltra Island

Cape Hammond

Sombrero Chino

Punta Mangle

Isabela

Eden Island

Gordon Rocks

Plazas Islands

Mariela Islets

Perry Isthmus

Cartago Bay

**Santa Cruz
Island**

Elizabeth Bay

Pinzon I.

Punta Pitt

Punta Moreno

Island

Nameless I.

San Cristobal Island

Kicker Rock

Caleta Webb

Sierra Negra

Tortuga Bay

Santa Fe Island

Punta Essex

Academy Bay

Puerto Ayora

Cerro Azul

Crossman Islands

Puerto Baquerizo Moreno

Caleta Iguana

Puerto Villamil

Ocean

Roca Union

Tortuga Island

South East Tradewinds

Punta Cormorant
Post Office Bay

Champion Island

Floreana Island

0 10 20 30 40 50   100 km

Puerto Velasco Ibarra

Enderby Island

Gardner Island

Watson Island

COPYRIGHT AUSTRALIAN GEOGRAPHIC PTY LTD

Punta Suarez

Gardner Bay

Española Island

Inset (top right)

CENTRAL AMERICA

Middle America Trench

0   600 km

COCOS

Cocos Island

P L A T E

Cocos Ridge

El Niño Flow

Malpelo Rock

Galapagos Spreading Centre

EQUATOR

Cromwell Current (Equatorial Countercurrent)

Carnegie Ridge

SOUTH

**Galapagos
Islands**

Galapagos
Platform

AMERICA

South Equatorial Current

Peru–Chile Trench

N A Z C A

Peru Oceanic Current

Humboldt Current (Peru Coastal Current)

P L A T E

South East Tradewinds

Predominant currents upwelling

Sunset over Mariela Islet, Elizabeth Bay, Isabela.

AUTHOR'S NOTE: A VISION OF WILDNESS
About this Book

Someone once said that life is what happens while you're busy making other plans. Perhaps. As I enter my sixth decade and I ask myself what in fact were my plans, or whether I could ever have been happy pursuing anything but nature photography, I realize that my destiny was charted long before I ever suspected it. The newlyweds back in 1952 — my parents — who pursued a vision of life far removed from the ravages of World War II or the spectres of European industry and pollution, unwittingly laid out that course. It was they, not I, who decided to leave Belgium to live in the Galapagos Islands, who had the steadfastness to turn dreams into reality, who confronted the anguish of adaptation to harsh new circumstances, and who made the immense sacrifice of saying farewell forever to friends and relatives. I only tottered along behind as an infant, never realizing the weight of such a decision, but revelling in the life of wonder and discovery that came with it. Through all my childhood years, I shared their fascination for all that was wild, those things that were new to them but encompassed the entire known world to me.

As I became a teenager I delighted in the earnest loan of my father's treasured antique camera. Many a late night was spent shining a battery-powered hand light through his home-made enlarger, then watching by the red-filtered glow of a kerosene lantern the carefully hoarded, long-dated chemicals play their magic over black-and-white prints of my beloved pelicans and iguanas.

Here, in the Galapagos, the first seeds of my life's vocation began to germinate. At the same time, at the age of eleven, I developed a passion for birdlife and decided I would someday become an ornithologist. I spent long days alone in a tiny row-boat searching deep quiet inlets, or scrambling through dense mangrove thickets locating the nests of warblers and night herons. I studied a breeding survey paper a passing scientist had left us, memorizing all the Latin names of the Galapagos bird species, and recorded my observations of eggs and chicks, hatching and fledging dates, in the only notebook I have ever kept. Then one day a thought hit me as clearly as a heavenly revelation: I would use a camera as the ultimate tool to record every aspect of the life cycle of every species in the islands, until I had catalogued their every last secret. Simple.

Four decades later, with a smile I scan through endless trays representing tens of thousands of slides, not only from Galapagos but of wild regions ranging from the Arctic to the Antarctic, and I realize that my childhood goal has not yet been fulfilled, the process still on-going.

My early photographic ambitions turned into a career quite by chance at the age of 19. Up until then photography had been nothing more than a hobby, which I funded by curing goat skins to sell to the rare tourists and, later, by striking out as a sailing yacht crewhand, guide and self-taught naturalist. That year I happened to meet Les Line, editor of *Audubon* magazine in New York, who was visiting the Galapagos and took an interest in my images, resulting in the publication of my first photo essay, including the magazine cover. Unbeknown to me at first, this event was to redefine the focus of my life, providing me with the justification for the only way of living I could ever imagine, away from human artifice, breathing the freedom of the wild denizens of the world's wildest places.

When I was offered the opportunity to produce this book, I realized the time had come to attempt to crystallize into one volume the near mythical status that the Galapagos have come to hold in the human psyche, not just in my own, but in those of all who have been touched by the islands' overwhelming magnetism through the ages. As I picked carefully through my photo collection and began to build word pictures to accompany the colour images, my soul soon drifted back to all of its old haunts. This is where my instincts were honed and my spirit roamed free for nearly four decades. This is where I became who I am, where

Sea lion playing in undersea grotto, northern coast, Seymour.

22

the present sometimes melds with eternity. I have arranged each group of photos with an accompanying chapter to emphasize one distinct aspect of the Galapagos and the striking natural contrasts that exist here, from the charged atmosphere of an active volcano to the silence of the mist-shrouded surrounding ocean which is home to numerous whales and schooling sharks; from the seasonal cycles of the ancient giant tortoises to the vibrant life of the seabird colonies on the outpost islands. Within each chapter are photos carefully chosen to stand alone in conveying the essence and moods of Galapagos, complemented by a small photo essay ending each section and designed to provide a glimpse of a story within the story. Only in this manner did I find it possible to expose the many layers of significance present within the Galapagos scene. Above all, this book is intended as a celebration of one of the world's unique natural gems, though I feel no amount of intimacy could ever lay bare all its secrets.

In the fast evolving world of professional nature photography it has become fashionable to speak of the photographs one 'makes', implying hard work, cold calculation and rigourous planning in the process of obtaining each image. I still feel I simply 'take' photos the old fashioned way: they are not created within my thought processes. Fleeting or enduring, the scenes are there in all their splendour and perfection, whether I or anyone else takes notice. Nor do I see my photography as work; it is simply my excuse to immerse myself deeper into nature, and it is the only way I know of sharing the love, trust and respect I feel for true wildness anywhere on this planet. All I do is capture the light of the moment, on a small scrap of celluloid made sensitive by modern technology. The joy I derive from revisiting the magic of those instants, treasuring them and sharing them with like-minded fellow humans cannot be measured or explained.

Together with my partner then, Mark Jones, who left his native England in pursuit of similar objectives as mine, I have continued to explore not only the many facets of Galapagos nature but also other pristine regions of the world. This has enabled me to gain perspective on the Galapagos scene and come to realize anew both the level of their incredible uniqueness and heart-rending fragility. Because of runaway progress and the politics that accompany explosive population growth, it has become almost impossible to live at peace with nature in the Galapagos. We therefore moved our home base to New Zealand to pursue our ideals, but a part of me will always remain on those untamed volcanic shores under the equatorial sunshine. I return frequently, and will treasure to the end of my days the understanding these islands have given me of the beauty and justice of nature.

The closing chapter in this book is dedicated to outlining the realities increasingly facing Galapagos. To anyone who has ever been touched by the Galapagos aura it is unthinkable that these islands should ever be lost to the world. Yet the tenuous balance between man and nature that was cautiously crafted in times past has been shaken to its very foundations and is in danger of vanishing irretrievably into history as every new day progresses. It is my fervent hope that this book, by encapsulating over half a century of Galapagos lore, and displaying visually the essence of its splendid wildness, can serve as an inspiration to ensure their survival.

No one in Galapagos, in Ecuador or in the world wants to see the Galapagos perish. What must be realized, however, is that the commitment to halt their demise will be exponentially tested with the passing of time.

Marine iguanas heading out to feed in early morning, Cape Douglas, Fernandina.

PROLOGUE: THE ESSENCE OF GALAPAGOS
A Personal Perspective

Like enraged demons, shapeless globs of glowing molten rock plunge writhing into the frothy grey sea. Jagged black fingers claw the shoreline. Fiery sparks fly and billows of purplish steam rise as red-hot lava cascades over the cliff edge. The restless volcanic spirits of Fernandina Island are on the prowl again, changing, reshaping the land. The last light of dusk is fading from the sky, but the deep sanguine glow in the atmosphere and the intense heat parching my face more than make up for the departed sunshine.

As I move away to cool off in the breeze, I realize that near my feet a scattering of marine iguanas, like so many dragons guarding this otherworldly scene, sit motionless along the same cliff edge where I was perching not ten metres from the flowing lava. Gentle seaweed eaters, they are helpless to understand the volcanic convulsions that are reshaping their native island. They stand with heads and bodies raised stiffly off the ground as they would at the height of noon, trying in vain to dispel heat in the breeze. A few hours ago I even saw several of these metre-long lizards inadvertently straying into the very path of the flowing lava, where they instantly burst into flames. This scene typifies how all life came to be moulded to the peculiar environment of the Galapagos Islands.

Enchanted isles lost in blue tropical seas; gigantic tortoises and flightless seabirds; scientific investigation and discoveries; human fortunes and human tragedies; the Galapagos have always meant very different things people through the centuries. Some have called them Hell on Earth, others, Paradise Lost. The man credited with their discovery, a seafaring Spanish bishop in 1535 named Fray Tomás de Berlanga who stumbled upon them while sailing from Panama to Peru, described the new islands as a place 'where God had showered the earth in stones... worthless'. To the renowned 19th-century American writer Herman Melville 'no spot on earth can in desolateness furnish a parallel to this group'. Even the eminent British naturalist Charles Darwin's first impression in 1835 compared the Galapagos to 'the cultivated parts of infernal regions'. Yet five weeks of observation and collection of their unique species was enough to form the basis of his landmark Theory of Evolution.

I was only two years old when my parents decided to make these wild volcanoes their home more than half a century ago. They arrived in the Galapagos Islands when almost no-one knew they even existed and raised their two children in the midst of nature. My earliest memories are of sunshine and endless beaches marked only by the footprints of turtles and seabirds, of diving among sea lions in search of abundant lobsters, of climbing volcanoes and helping my father hunt wild goats for the dinner table. I wore no shoes and few clothes, knew no electricity or running water, but life was rich beyond measure. The Galapagos Islands were my classroom throughout my learning years. I saw my first automobile when I was ten. In my late teens I was offered an opportunity to attend college in California, but opted instead for a short visit, and to continue exploring my own islands. Their wildness and harmony has etched into my spirit a profound respect and abiding love for the natural world, and has given me my career as a nature photographer and writer. Today, I feel I know their moods and secrets as intimately as if they were a kindred spirit.

Cursed, revered or ruthlessly exploited, the Galapagos have always attracted passionate feelings. Pirates, convicts, mystics, pioneers, explorers, scientists, heads of state and royalty, all have trodden their forbidding shores. The motivations driving this odd sampling of humanity have been as widely differing as their status, from banishment by political enemies to the simple desire to commune with nature, and from religious impulses to megalomaniac financial enterprise. I feel most content to have been one of the pioneering families who have dedicated their life to carving a niche for themselves in harmony with nature. My brother was born in Galapagos, and my father is buried in their volcanic soil. To me Galapagos is still a place where the earth is at peace with itself, and man is only a guest — a colourful, turbulent guest who must learn the hard way to respect the environment. Galapagos is timeless — man, in his hurried lifetime, only passes through.

Overleaf: *Dawn over Alcedo Volcano, giant tortoises in rainy season pool, Isabela.*

Pelican and booby on jagged lava shoreline at sunrise, Urvina Bay, Isabela.

1 THE TEST OF TIME
The Historical Context

Stark volcanoes straddling the equatorial line about 1,000 kilometres from the west coast of South America, alone in the vast eastern Pacific Ocean, the Galapagos Islands are a geographical anomaly on a world scale — geologically, biologically, climatically, historically and socially. To begin with, the geologic origin of the Galapagos is something of a mystery. Made up of 15 main islands and several dozen smaller ones, the archipelago does not form part of any major land mass, and has never done so. The islands rise steeply from the ocean floor, huge active shield volcanoes (low-angled, shield-shaped, basaltic oceanic volcanoes similar to those in Hawaii) clustered atop the massive submarine Galapagos Platform. They are the result of what is known as a geologic 'hotspot', where a stationary thermal plume rising from deep within the earth's mantle relentlessly builds up volcanoes on the overlying tectonic plate as it drifts slowly above. The Nazca Plate on which the Galapagos ride moves east-south-east at a rate of just a few centimetres per year. As the islands age they are carried away from the hotspot on this geological conveyor belt, their volcanoes gradually dying and eroding, eventually sinking back into the sea. Although the oldest islands still standing today are likely to be no more than three to five million years old, it is possible that many older islands have disappeared in the distant past, as the hotspot has continuously nurtured the growth of new volcanoes in the wake of dying islands. The recent discovery of sunken sea mounts, as well as the presence of the submarine Carnegie Ridge leading like a tell-tale trail all the

In the early 1980s a new lake formed inside the caldera of Cerro Azul, Isabela.

way to the Peru-Chile Trench, where the Pacific Ocean floor is subducted beneath the South American continent, suggest this process may have been at work for tens of millions of years.

The western islands are the youngest, their newly formed volcanoes standing naked in the blazing sun, building more land with every new eruption. Here I witnessed Fernandina Volcano's latest outburst, in 1995, and have seen, year after year, the ever-changing faces of an island still in its youthful formation. To the south-east lie the older islands, where erosion and the passage of time have allowed a gentle cloak of vegetation to soften their basaltic contours. On these islands fresh water is available, allowing the establishment of human settlements, such as Academy Bay, on Santa Cruz Island, where I grew up. The climate of the Galapagos is exceptional, considering their tropical position. Cold oceanic upwellings from the west, surging up from the deepest layers of the equatorial Pacific, combine with further upwelling currents flowing up the coast of South America to bring an arid, cool climate to the coastal regions of the islands.

Our coolest season is during the northern summer, when wind and

Land iguana and Galapagos doves living in arid cactus forest, Santa Fe.

A sudden flush of growth follows the first El Niño rains; land iguana eating Portulaca blossoms, Plazas.

cloud cover are frequent but rain does not fall at lower elevations. This is known locally as the *garua* season, referring to the fine drizzle that may sweep in daily from the sea between July and November, but does nothing more than dampen the surface of the lava. By contrast, the rainy season from January to March is short, hot and totally unpredictable. For the rains to develop, the tradewinds that drive the cool currents must slacken sufficiently to allow warm waters to flow down from the Panama region, bringing with them high sea temperatures and heavy precipitation typical of tropical areas and known to sailors as 'the doldrums'. In some years these warm waters never reach Galapagos, in others they may flood as far south as Peru, causing a phenomenon known as El Niño. This time of year was a source of great expectation during my childhood, waiting for signs of black thunderclouds, and the sudden flush of greenery that soon swept across the otherwise desert landscape. If the rains failed, all terrestrial creatures were stressed to the utmost, land iguanas on small islands starving during the long drought and land birds not even attempting to nest, while for people this meant dry water tanks and having to rely entirely on brackish water to drink. Yet during a severe El Niño year it would be the marine

species that would suffer from the loss of life-giving cold currents.

For most of the islands rising above 400 to 500 metres a totally different climatic zone prevails. Thick blankets of near-constant mist clinging to their upper slopes generate a lush montane forest on many of the older islands, where vermilion flycatchers flit among mosses and orchids, and owls hunt flightless rails.

The combination of a unique climate and the swift, nutrient-rich ocean currents that bathe the islands nurture an environment that is as remarkable in the sea as it is on land. There is not a doubt that from the very first time man set eyes on the Galapagos to the present day, what has impressed everyone, without fail, is the strangeness of the animals that abound on the virgin shores, from the prehistoric giant tortoises to the little finches that now bear Darwin's name. The isolation of the islands, and time for life to evolve and adapt in an environment where no continental predators ever existed, culminated in species which were as bizarre as they were unafraid when the first people arrived. In the first written account of Galapagos, in 1535, Tomás de Berlanga speaks of 'many seals, turtles, iguanas and birds, but so silly they do not know how to flee'.

The vast majority of Galapagos reptiles and land birds are endemic to the islands. Even within the archipelago there are different species limited to one island each. From lava lizards to mockingbirds, land species that were isolated on single islands evolved differently from their neighbours, each representing a classic case of what is known to biologists as 'adaptive radiation'. This is an example of one species which through time has adapted to match the particular conditions of its own environment, producing a new species on each island. This situation is what has earned the Galapagos the title of 'Natural Laboratory of Evolution' and has attracted the attention of scientists from Darwin's day onward.

The highlight of scientific investigation today is none other than the group of 13 closely related species of Darwin's finches, actually some of the least noticeable Galapagos birds. Common throughout all of the islands, with unpretentious songs and drab black and brown plumage, each type has adapted to best take advantage of a distinct food source. Yet they are still so similar to each other that they are incredibly difficult to tell apart, a case of evolution in progress. An on-going study of Darwin's finches

Cool currents bathe the shores in garua season mist while blue-footed boobies nest during this time of marine productivity, Punta Vicente Roca, Isabela.

conducted by Drs Peter and Rosemary Grant, spanning over two decades, has seen evolutionary science propelled from simple taxonomy into the age of computer analysis and genetic fingerprinting. Their conclusions, recently published, have been no less startling: far from being a gradual development spread over geologic time, evolution among Darwin's finches is a dynamic

food supply. For 18 years she returned, establishing a longevity record for her species at the time.

It is said that Galapagos has one of the best studied biota in the world. Drawing highly respected researchers from all over the globe, detailed studies have covered everything from blind cave spiders to the pollination process

A rare tool-using adaptation in birds, a woodpecker finch uses a cactus spine to prise out a grub, Santa Cruz.

process, redefined and reoriented from year to year, with substantial adaptations appearing throughout an entire island population in response to short-term climatic trends. Erratic weather patterns spread over just a few years — very much a hallmark of the Galapagos environment — are sufficient to cause major reversals in natural selection, favouring subtle genetic traits within only a few generations of birds.

Even from a non-scientific point of view the little Darwin's finches are a source of much fascination. Bold and inquisitive like all other Galapagos wildlife, they flock into people's houses and soon learn where the easiest feeding opportunities can be found. When I was seven years old I tamed a young cactus finch by offering breadcrumbs in my hand. This finch, a female, later brought her mate and her babies, year after year, to feed from our fingers. She learned that the bread was kept inside the house and would sit by the door rattling the insect screens and making as much noise as possible to attract attention and be allowed to come in. Or she would sit on our heads, flying back and forth to the door, either to come in or to leave again when she had finished feeding. In years of drought she was the only bird in the vicinity who was able to raise young thanks to her private

of native plants, from the breeding biology of flightless cormorants to the diving physiology of marine iguanas. To this day the biology of the Galapagos Islands remains in something of a time capsule, a small sample of prehistoric days cast adrift through the ages, largely bypassed by the impact of humanity until recent years.

From the cultural point of view the islands are also an anachronism, being one of the largest groups in the tropical Pacific Ocean that was never colonized by early Polynesians. While all other major islands, from Hawaii to Easter Island, Tahiti to New Zealand, gave rise to one insular civilization after another, causing waves of extinction among endemic species across the Pacific, Galapagos remained the realm of reptiles and birds. Even though Berlanga is credited with the first landfall in 1535, he may not in fact have been the true discoverer. An Inca legend of pre-Colombian days tells of a voyage made by one of their leaders to a group of distant islands. Tupac Yupanqui, travelling with a fleet of balsa rafts, is said to have named one of them 'Island of Fire' after its smouldering summit — probably an erupting

A marine iguana at home on the salt-sprayed lava shore, Punta Suarez, Española.

Swallow-tailed gulls roost along the surf-beaten cliff, Punta Suarez, Española.

A young fur seal and a blue-footed booby, Cape Douglas, Fernandina.

volcano. After many months he returned to South America bearing, among other things, 'the hide of a horse' and a 'bronze chair'. These items, through the interpretation of oral history, may well have started life as a sea lion's skin and the saddle-like carapace of a giant tortoise, which we must remember in later years was given the name of a Spanish saddle, *galápago*.

Neither the Incas nor Berlanga, however, spent much time on the wild Galapagos shores. For over 150 years after the Bishop's landing only sporadic Spanish sailing vessels passed by the islands. Almost invariably they had been swept helplessly out to sea while plying coastal shipping routes, carried off course by the same currents that give the islands their unusual climate. Becalmed in clumsy wind-powered ships and desperate for drinking water, these early sailors watched one island after another drift in and out of the mists, seemingly travelling at will across the horizon, and concluded they were only ghosts, dubbing them 'The Enchanted Isles'.

Not until the end of the 17th century did the human history of Galapagos begin in earnest, and with it the imprint of man's first impact upon their natural balance. First came a motley band of daring opportunists, ruthless soldiers of fortune intent on plundering the Spanish port cities along the South American coast, or intercepting treasure galleons

carrying gold and silver from Peru. British buccaneers and later privateers all capitalized on the Spaniards' incredulity of the Galapagos Islands' existence, using their sheltered bays as convenient hideaways to restore their ships between forays. Later came whalers in search of oil to fuel the industrial revolutions of Europe and North America, and on their heels, sealers seeking their fortunes in furs from the endemic Galapagos fur seal.

What all these early visitors had in common was a great taste for the fresh meat of the giant tortoise, which could be kept alive in the holds of sailing ships for months without food or water, providing fresh meat for the sailors during long ocean crossings. They scoured the mountains for the ancient tortoises and carried them away by the hundreds of thousands, totalling perhaps fifty or more times the number that still survive today. At the same time many domestic animals, from cats and dogs to pigs, goats and cattle, were released or escaped on the islands, reproducing fast and beginning the slow destruction of the natural habitat. Over the centuries the islands suffered greatly, and a number of species became extinct, some

On a cool morning Galapagos hawks are attracted to warm sulphur fumaroles inside the caldera, Alcedo Volcano, Isabela.

A young pelican perching amid basking marine iguanas, Punta Espinosa, Fernandina.

before any scientist had ever seen them, such as the giant rodent *Megaoryzomis*, leaving only bones to tell their tale.

Still humanity was only passing, there were no Galapagos natives. The first hesitant settlers appeared about the beginning of the 19th century, lone marooned sailors and other mysterious misfits, none of whom stayed long. In the year 1832, only three years before Darwin's celebrated visit, the newly independent Republic of Ecuador laid formal claim to the Galapagos Archipelago, backing a colony made up of mutinous soldiers and political prisoners under the tyrannical leadership of an army colonel. This was to start a trend of slavery, rebellion and murder which lasted well into the 20th century. Criminals and political adversaries were regularly banished to the islands, providing the labour for the dreams of self-made emperors who sought to enrich themselves through the exploitation of natural resources, from lichens for the textile dye industry to sulphur from active volcanoes. But each one of these ventures ended in tragedy, the prisoners leaving their bones along the desolate shores, sometimes joined by those of their merciless bosses. There were even negotiations between the governments of Ecuador and the United States to capitalize on hypothetical riches in guano, estimated in the millions of dollars, but what no-one realized at the time is that the Galapagos volcanic shores harbour no guano reserves.

Meanwhile, the Galapagos had already captured the attention of scientists and a leisure class of explorers around the world, many of whom mounted private expeditions and publicized the islands' uniqueness. This in turn attracted a collection of colonists during the first half of this century, people with visions and skills that enabled them not only to survive, but sometimes even to thrive. Thus for the first time in history, a true breed of Galapagos citizen was born. Fishermen came from the coast of Ecuador and farmers from the Andes. Dreamers and free spirits escaped Europe during the throes of two world wars. One mystic came to practice eastern religion long before this became fashionable in western countries. A colonizing venture in 1926 brought a Norwegian fishing cooperative, another as late as 1959, an American communal coffee plantation scheme. Only a few of these settlers were successful, many ending in ignominious failure. In the 1930s a gun-toting baroness, self-proclaimed Empress of Floreana Island, and her two lovers disappeared without a trace, leaving behind a mystery that has not been solved to this day, while at the same time an eccentric vegetarian dentist apparently died of food poisoning after eating, of all things, potted chicken. In 1956 a lone American attempted to evade his own predictions of a global nuclear holocaust by going to live in total isolation on an active volcano, only to die of excessive alcohol consumption, the drink supplied by passing fishing boats.

Beside the utopians and misfits lived a slowly growing group of hard-working, peace-loving pioneers who painstakingly cleared the land and planted crops of coffee, bananas, avocados and vegetables, hunted feral goats and cattle, or fished the abundant grouper and lobsters. They raised and educated their children, some of whom were later to have Galapagos children of their own. These are the days that I recall. My father, like others, fished and salted his catch to export on the occasional ship that came from the mainland of Ecuador. Two, three, six months might pass before one of these small freighters would appear on the horizon, the only contact with the outside world. With it came letters from families far away, and vital supplies such as candles, flour and sugar. When it left a few days later it took away the dried fish, dried coffee and live cattle that were the inhabitants' only source of cash. Life was hard, simple and beautiful back then. One time the freighter failed to come for several months and everyone on the island ran out of matches, making it imperative to keep their fires alive, in the spirit of stone age cavemen. Everyone was healthy, for you could not afford to fall ill where there was no doctor. An itinerant dentist visited for one month and made his fortune.

My family eked out a living from small sporadic exports like the other pioneers, by share-harvesting the coffee crop, fishing or diving for lobsters. Later we turned to collecting insects, sea shells and other marine invertebrates for scientists and museums abroad. My father taught himself how to build a rowing-boat, used for fishing and fetching water from the opposite side of the bay in barrels and buckets. This was followed by a motor boat to explore the other islands, and eventually a seagoing sailing yacht which gave us greater mobility and was occasionally chartered out to small parties and visitors. In the late 1960s the first regular tourists arrived and my parents turned their creative skills to producing souvenirs such as hand-painted postcards and handcrafted jewellery depicting the native wildlife.

When I was 14 I left the Galapagos for the first time, travelling with my mother on a small freighter for the five day crossing, along with a multitude of cattle, pigs, chickens and large families with small children crowding the decks, to reach the port city of Guayaquil. I enjoyed the sights and sounds of high-rise buildings, neon signs and city traffic, but was relieved to catch the return ship back to our island one month later. The year was 1968 and change was in the air. Our largest volcano, Fernandina, erupted spectacularly. The following year I acquired my first professional camera. Planes began to reach the islands, occasional charters at first, then regular tourist flights. A new era had begun.

Fernandina sunrise, sea lions and Galapagos hawk, Punta Espinosa.

Vulcanism

The shield volcanoes of Isabela and Fernandina are among the most active in the world, with eruptions redesigning the contours of the islands frequently. Numerous parasitic cones build along both rim fissures (top left, Volcan Chico, Sierra Negra, 1979) and flank faults (bottom left, Cerro Azul, 1979). Fluid basalt flows in lava rivers (right top) that boil the sea when they reach the coast (bottom right), while spatter cones build around the vents (far right, all three Fernandina 1995). The sounds, smells and constant movement of these grandest of natural spectacles overwhelm all senses.

A peaceful warm-season sunrise over Tortuga Bay beach, visited often in my childhood, Santa Cruz.

2 CHILDHOOD ENCHANTMENTS
Galapagos Discoveries

Stars by the millions danced overhead as our small boat, my family's tiny floating home, rocked contentedly in the intimate confines of a lava-studded cove. Rambunctious young sea lions chased each other and leapt all around us, blowing bubbles under the hull and occasionally landing a shower of cold salt spray over the railing, only inches above sea-level. The dinner dishes, rinsed in the sea, lay stacked unceremoniously to dry in a plastic bucket in the cockpit. Our single kerosene storm-lantern was blown out as my Mom and young brother retreated to the relative comfort of the minuscule fore cabin for the night. My Dad, over six feet tall, folded himself in amongst the fuel and water drums, sundry gear and provisions that were to keep the family alive for weeks at a time, burrowing down into the dry cosiness of what was grandly called the aft cabin.

My digs, too, were in the aft cabin, but fearful that I should miss out on some detail of the magical Galapagos night, I always made the deck my sleeping quarters. I spread out my bedroll across the deck in a well-rehearsed routine, lay down without undressing and rolled over several times until well trussed in my cotton blanket. Fourteen years old and growing fast, my feet touched the port railing, my pillow protruding over the water to starboard. I could hear the plaintive bleatings of a newborn sea lion on the beach, the cheerful trills of a pair of oystercatchers in a duet, and the distant, mysterious screech of an owl somewhere over the island. The heavy, salty dew soaked slowly through my covers and tousled hair. 'I don't understand',

Sea turtles among schooling creole fish were exciting snorkelling encounters, Devil's Crown, Floreana.

an expert in her own right, mapping the habitat of most Galapagos molluscs and referencing new species down to family and genus. We probed reefs and tide pools and snorkelled as deep as a single breath would allow. My father, André, built a wire mesh dredge and hand-crank winch which could be dropped to over 200 metres. For hours on end he and I would work the twin winch handles, bent double at the stern of the boat, while my mother steered slowly in reverse. Almost every haul brought up species never seen before, many amazingly delicate and intricate in design. In due course experts described them as new species, the type specimens, or prototypes, lodged in the American Museum of Natural History, Los Angeles County Museum and elsewhere. *Fissurela andrei, Murexiella jacquelinae, Strombina deroyana, Latiaxis santacruzensis* and many more, all resulted from those heady days.

In many ways the pursuit of sea shells only served to fuel an even greater passion, that of simple exploration, to give free rein to one's curiosity about the natural world. The financial rewards of the sea shells had allowed the replacement of our first tiny boat, the *Puck*, for the relative comfort and seaworthiness of the *Kim*. The first boat had been built the year after my brother was born by my father's two hands and a small hoard of tools brought from Belgium. It was just five metres long, powered by a home-made sail and a three horsepower engine, but too small to shelter people or gear from drenching rain or salt spray. On our short forays to other islands we had to camp ashore among the sea lions, the *Puck* tethered to the coastline by a long rope lest its anchor should break loose and leave us marooned. The *Kim*, on the other hand, seven metres long, of double-planked oak and with a seven horsepower diesel, had been purchased in the mid-60s from a disillusioned German dentist who'd returned to his homeland after his Galapagos pioneering dreams had turned to dust in just a couple of years. Refurbished, this boat now offered us all the basic safety, self-sufficiency and rudimentary living space to explore the islands to our hearts' content.

Our first outings were tentative, venturing not much further down the coast of Santa Cruz Island than we already had by rowing boat or on foot. An old island, sleeping peacefully through time, its long-still volcanoes cloaked in vegetation, Santa Cruz offered endless rewards and closely guarded secrets. Eagerly we coaxed our prow into every cove and inlet, from the surf-beaten reefs of the south coast to the sheltered north shore decorated with sparkling white beaches and jade-coloured mangrove

my father would say resignedly, as he did every night at my rejection of the snug dryness of my allotted bunk, his words trailing off unfinished since he could find no convincing argument: a little wind and seawater had never killed anyone.

My mother's last act of the day had been to bring out the family's most precious possession, a small, portable record-player a long lost friend had shipped through the mail as a gift from Belgium. From the transistor machine gently wedged on a folded blanket against the rolling wave action, the ethereal notes of Bach, Vivaldi, Beethoven and Mozart filled the Galapagos night for as long as the six D-cells lasted. The full moon rose in an explosion of light, drowning out the stars. Sea lion and seabird voices mingled with the clear notes of violin and piano. Sleep came easily to someone beginning to think about growing up.

These were golden years. My family had met amazing success with their specimen sea shell business, which soon turned into a passion. Researchers, museum curators, collectors and shell clubs from all over the world were writing with questions and requests. My mother, Jacqueline, by corresponding with many museum specialists she had never met, became

A green turtle buries her eggs at sunrise before slipping back to the sea, Bartolome.

lagoons. Often I begged my parents to let me walk the coast alone while they motored to the next anchorage several miles away. My lone footprints would wend their way among sea turtle nests on pristine beaches, or through the pink and brown mud flats fringing flamingo lagoons. I found watering holes frequented by wild donkeys, colonies of pelicans, or shards of pottery where buccaneers had once camped. Once I brought home the rare prize of a decorative glass fishing float, cast ashore, laden with barnacles after its oceanwide drift. But my main obsession was in discovering nesting birds, from yellow warblers to great blue herons.

For my brother, Gil, fascination lay in ferreting out marine fossils deposited in layers of raised seafloor sediments, sandwiched between lava flows at the base of various cliffs. The delicate curled imprints of early sea shells took him back a million years or more to unknown Galapagos beginnings. Alone or together, we pursued our explorations with the joy and innocence of true discovery. From a clifftop we heard our first fur seals, eerie screams that brought visions of forlorn shipwrecked sailors. Whenever possible we also investigated inland regions, led by my father's insatiable

Cactus-studded channels offered endless explorations, Academy Bay, Santa Cruz.

Flamingos sometimes flew past travelling from one bay to another, Floreana.

Brown pelicans nesting in the mangroves of Academy Bay, Santa Cruz.

desire to examine the minute, barely noticeable details of landscape and life forms. Through the cactus forests and over lava fields we hiked, seeking panoramic views from the tops of small volcanic cones, or following cliff lines running far inland. Craters and sometimes pools were spied, and an underground network of lava tubes where, amazingly, brackish groundwater harboured a tiny, blind, pigment-free cave fish new to science.

Sometimes, especially when the sea was rough and uninviting, we eschewed boat travel and donned backpacks for camping explorations of the highlands. Here we wandered over rolling bracken fields, and through deep, moisture-laden cloud forests of *Miconia* and *Scalesia* festooned with green-flowered orchids and gold and brown liverworts. Endemic flightless rails flitted underfoot between clumps of grass and delicate stands of *Lycopodium* mosses. Vermilion flycatchers perched on giant tree ferns and short-eared owls hunted by day in the low mist. At every stop my father turned over logs and stones and searched the undergrowth for small endemic land snails, soon discovering that each and every landmark, hillock, valley or even stand of trees, yielded its own distinct species. Few had ever been collected and he eventually amassed several dozen different types, each carefully labelled with date and location.

But even as he went on finding new forms, already something strange was happening to these modest examples of island evolution. In many areas only dead, fading shells could be found scattered under every bush, sometimes in great heaps. It was the first sign of a great unexplained wave of extinction that swept through the land snail population across the entire island in the '60s and '70s. Today, the last of their bleached shells are turning to dust, my father's collections and those of a handful of dedicated scientists now scattered in museums round the world, all that remains of what may have been a story in evolution and adaptive radiation every bit as fascinating as that of Darwin's finches.

When the seas grew calm and warm, emboldened by time and experience, we began taking the *Kim* to islands further afield, first the satellite islets around Santa Cruz: Eden with its tiny olivine beach and its amphitheatre of scrub-covered, ochre coloured tuff (rock formed by volcanic ash); Daphne, a larger symmetrical tuff cone with steep flanks and a deep crater where blue-footed boobies nested; Baltra, flat, red-rocked and sunbaked, but fringed with turtle nesting beaches, an island harbouring the odd relics of a United States Air Force presence during World War II and later to know the hubbub of tourist flights; Mosquera, a white, sandy

The clear waters of Santa Fe's only bay attract schools of spotted eagle rays.

jewel covered in noisy sea lions; Seymour, resembling Baltra, but home to nesting boobies and frigates; Plazas, a magical place we visited many times, where over 1,000 sea lions fought, played and slept, crowded along the lava shore, where gleaming tropic birds and nocturnal swallow-tailed gulls wheeled and courted by the windy cliffside, and proud stands of reddish-barked cacti enticed land iguanas and cactus finches to vie for their sweet but prickly yellow blossoms.

Eventually we pushed on to Santa Fe Island, 30 kilometres to the east of our home. Its emerald bay was alive with sea lions we loved for their indomitable playfulness, but also distrusted deeply for their mock charges that successfully sent us scampering from the oh-so-beckoning clear shallows. A small islet protecting the bay and thickly forested with giant *Opuntia* cacti, revealed numerous secretive nesting Galapagos doves and night herons, and kindled my early enthusiasm for keeping bird notes. Expectant Galapagos hawks followed us on hunting trips into the arid interior of the island where herds of feral goats had created a cactus studded

San Cristobal is one of the older islands, where time has allowed erosion to carve the ancient tuff cones, Punta Pitt.

parkland before their successful eradication in 1972. A rare treat in those days was to spot the pale lumbering form of a long-suffering land iguana, a species found only on this island and, unlike the now vanished giant tortoises, surviving in spite of the goat ravages.

Beyond Santa Fe we reached the easternmost island of San Cristobal, and to the south-west, Floreana. Like Santa Cruz, both islands were old, sprinkled with clusters of extinct volcanic cones and mostly covered in dormant vegetation awaiting the fickle rains. San Cristobal revealed turquoise bays, turtle nesting beaches and grandly sculpted ancient tuff cones, where wind and wave had gouged fissures and tunnels in the soft volcanic ash. Towering pale cliffs and echoing caverns above water gave way to multicoloured gardens of sea fans and cup corals below. On Floreana, parasitic cones dotted the island generously from the interior to the coast in reds, browns and black, sheltering multihued beaches and tranquil flamingo lagoons. The miniature volcanoes even marched out to sea in a variety of intriguing tiny islands: Devil's Crown, aptly named spires marking the rim of a small submerged crater where sea lions and reef fish darted among one of the islands' rare coral reef formations; Champion, a symmetrical spatter cone where a sturdy race of giant cacti harboured a remnant population of the endemic Floreana mockingbird, plus nesting blue-footed boobies and swallow-tailed gulls; Enderby, named after the whalers of yore, a perfect pyramid dotted with the scarlet balloons of courting frigate birds like so many glowing fruits among the stunted vegetation; Gardner, monolithic, a favourite place to find lobsters along its undercut submarine walls; Watson, pale and guano splattered, carved by the ocean, with giant arches giving it the uncanny silhouette of a monstrous elephant.

Floreana and San Cristobal each had their own human settlements as well but, like Santa Cruz, the majority of the land, especially the coast, remained relatively unscarred. Each had its own species of lava lizards and mockingbirds, and its own flavour that makes every island in the Galapagos as distinct from its neighbours as each person in a large family is different from all brothers and sisters.

Flamingos were among the shiest wildlife before they became accustomed to seeing people, Rabida.

Overleaf: *The panoramic view from the top of Bartolome Island is unsurpassed on a clear sunrise.*

45

Santiago is a blend of old and new land, vegetation-covered cones surrounded by sterile lava fields, Sullivan Bay.

Flamingo lagoons always offered an idyllic touch amid the sere volcanic surroundings, Rabida.

Travelling north from Santa Cruz we investigated the other neighbouring islands. In contrast with the southern islands, here we seemed to take a leap through time, with many signs of recent volcanic activity, shiny black lava flows overlaying older rusty-coloured ones, which in turn surrounded 'islands' of weathered, vegetation-covered terrain. Santiago was an island of contrasts which invited exploration, as did its picturesque satellite islets: Bartolome with its golden beaches, moonlike craters and graceful Pinnacle Rock. And Sombrero Chino, 'Chinese Hat', a perfect little volcano complete with lava flows, lava tubes and an impressive crater, on the rim of which grew diminutive lava cacti, *Brachycereus*, one of the first life forms to colonize new volcanic ground.

Nearby lay Rabida, steep and rugged, with only one beach of dark red sand. There, one evening, we spied a Galapagos snake eating a hapless marine iguana, in amongst the sleeping sea lions, next to a flamingo lagoon. Substantially larger, but equally steep, rocky and scrub covered, was Pinzon Island. Around its thorn-strangled crater, where rain rarely fell but mist often floated, ambled a remnant population of bizarre-looking, saddleback tortoises. Flared, raised shells and long slender legs and necks allowed them to browse for scanty foliage and juicy cactus pads, a resource that would remain beyond reach of conventional shaped tortoises found on greener islands.

The subtle seasons carried their surprises. January usually started with its flurry of mating turtles, schooling rays and pupping sharks all gathering in the seclusion of mangrove inlets, soon followed by hundreds of caterpillar-like tracks of nesting female turtles venturing nightly up the beaches. February to March, with luck, brought rains that burst upon the thirsty land, each shower within days painting a fresh green swathe of growth across the silvery *palo santo* forests, where finches, mockingbirds and warblers raised strings of noisy babies. April was when the waters cooled, the breeze and clear skies returned, fish schools moved inshore and pelicans and herons began to nest. By May to June adorable marine iguana hatchlings were scampering everywhere and armfuls of baby sea turtles erupted from nest-cratered beaches, attracting predatory frigates from afar. Come July

Living on a thorn scrub island, the Pinzon 'saddleback' tortoise can browse high in arid vegetation.

48

Never common, Galapagos penguins depend on baitfish schools forming in coastal shallows, Sombrero Chino.

and August the full force of the south-east tradewinds swept damply across the islands, cold upwellings nurturing marine life beyond measure, sea lions were fat and happy, seabirds of all types raised fluffy chicks, even whales converged on the rich green plankton soup that swirled in giant eddies driven by powerful currents. September to October marked the peak of the cold *garua* season: the bountiful sea rumbled and roared under constant grey skies while the islands slumbered, their summits shrouded in mist, the lowlands leafless, dormant, salt-scoured.

With November came the first signs of change once again with young seabirds everywhere starting to fledge and head offshore as the pattern of nutrient rich currents began to slacken. December was a time of expectation, the seas calming and clearing as winds dropped and plankton blooms vanished. Darwin's finches sang and pretended to build nests, people prayed and scrubbed out their empty rainwater tanks, scanning the now sunny skies for the first billowing clouds that would herald a long-awaited downpour. Sometimes these came by Christmas, other years the

When fish are close inshore pelicans gather to feed, Tortuga Bay, Santa Cruz.

The grey but rainless garua season is when boobies and other seabirds raise well-fed chicks, Daphne.

months passed without relief, until the cold season returned and brought freshness, even if no water, to the parched coastal regions.

Still, our wanderings thus far carried us only to the central part of the archipelago. In the unknown zone lay the outer islands: the towering western shield volcanoes of Isabela and Fernandina Islands, where to this day the Galapagos continue to be born in sporadic, convulsive outpourings of magma. Distant and mysterious were the thriving seabird islands of Española or Genovesa, and more so the outpost sentinels of Wolf and Darwin far to the north. All of these wonders, by which the central islands would almost seem to pale, awaited the days of my later teens when I turned my attention to guiding visitors on slightly larger boats, and especially the construction of yet another family boat, the ten metre *Inti*, lap-strake hulled and sloop-rigged, conceived, designed and built at home.

A green turtle returns to its element on Punta Cormorant, Floreana.

Dry and Humid Habitats

Lowland habitat (*this page*) All coastal regions, generally below 400 metres elevation, are typified by arid habitat where most of the vegetation remains leafless during the entire garua season. Dominated by two forms of giant cacti, Opuntia and Jasminocereus (*right*), this is where most of Darwin's ground finches live (*cactus finch, below*), along with mockingbirds, doves, hawks, lava lizards, snakes, land iguanas and saddleback tortoises on some islands.

Highland habitat (*facing page*) This humid environment is only found on islands high enough to capture the full effect of the humid tradewinds year round on their upper, south-facing flanks. On the older islands such as Santa Cruz (*top, far right*) misty summits and fern-draped cloud forests are home to tree and warbler finches, vermilion flycatchers (*centre right*), flightless rails, barn and short-eared owls (*bottom, far right*) and dome type tortoises. Tree ferns, epiphytic orchids and endemic land snails are but a few of the unique species found here.

Mangrove Habitat

Even where the land consists of no more than sun-baked lava flows, many sheltered bays are bordered by lush growth of four types of mangrove where the tangled aerial roots of the red mangrove dominate (right, above and below water). These areas act as nurseries for birds and fish alike. Egrets and herons, from little lava herons and secretive night herons to great blues (far right) nest and fish here, as do brown pelicans (below). Green turtles (right, below), golden rays (far right, below) and white-tipped reef sharks rest in their quiet seclusion, while in the warm season many fish come here to spawn and blacktip sharks to pup. Exploring these tranquil, glaucous waters is full of surprises.

The red-billed tropic bird, like other pelagic seabirds, approaches land only to nest, Genovesa.

3 SPIRITS OF THE TRADEWINDS

Winged Visitors from the Ocean Wide

The month was September, the dankest, coolest month of the year, when the unrelenting south-east tradewinds blow unwaveringly for weeks, carrying with them thousands of miles' worth of salty sea moisture before they hit land. On this late afternoon in 1991 I sat on the towering, south-facing cliff edge of Española Island, which is the first to face the prevailing weather. It was neither my first nor last visit to this wild and wonderful location, but it does remain one of my most memorable. Somewhere on the sheltered side of the island our sailboat *Inti* was anchored, already in her 15th year of Galapagos explorations. To windward, clammy strands of rainless clouds, typical of the *garua* season, blew low over the island's leafless scrubland, painted pale grey with encrusted lichens.

Slanting rays of pale golden sun danced on the scrabbly sea, while long, slow swells unleashed their oceanwide momentum in plumes of spray along the cliff face below.

Through this peaceful, primal scene, hundreds upon hundreds of seabirds floated like clouds of confetti, reeling, gliding, swooping, screaming, courting. The grandest of them all was the waved albatross, a rare bird numbering only about 12,000 pairs for the entire species, yet concentrated here as they streamed in from the ocean to their only nesting colony in the world (save for a few strays occasionally found on the small island of La Plata off the coast of Ecuador). With a wingspan of 2.4 metres it is not a very large albatross, and unlike many of its brethren, it does not frequent

Long ocean swells spend their force on the south facing cliffs of Española, home of the waved albatross.

the stormy seas around Antarctica. Instead it favours the rich, cold waters stretching to the south-east, nurtured by the upwellings of the Humboldt Current surging from the deep Peru-Chile Trench. Neither storms nor calm disrupt the stability of the weather here, nor does the wind so much as waver or change direction for months at a time. The waved albatross, its bright yellow beak and sulphur-tinged head unmistakable, glides effortlessly on the tradewinds and returns unfailingly to nest on this, the southernmost and oldest island of the Galapagos.

Indeed Española is a classic beacon island to all manner of seabirds. This flat-topped, modestly sized island is of great appeal to so many seabirds for the simple reason that it is the first speck of land they encounter across the vast tracts of ocean bordering the west coast of South America. For that tribe of birds known as true pelagics — those ocean wanderers whose

As the grasses dry, albatross and other ocean wanderers return to Española.

A red-billed tropic bird flies in from the high seas to search for cliff-face nesting cavities, Daphne.

Swallow-tailed gulls feed in the open ocean at night, visiting their nests on exposed cliffs by day, Wolf.

life is dictated by the patterns of winds and currents — land has but one attraction: to provide a firm, though temporary, base on which to hatch their eggs and raise their young. A predator-free island on the fringe of an oceanic archipelago could not better fit the bill. As soon as the nesting season is complete both adults and young leave the land for the open sea, often without so much as a backward glance until a new cycle begins.

That afternoon on the cliff edge, the bird traffic before me was a mesmerizing carousel of sound and motion swirling on the wind. Weaving across the rigid-winged gliding path of the albatross, bands of shimmering white, fast-flapping red-billed tropic birds cruised to and fro, courting on the wing. In groups of two to five, or sometimes up to a dozen, they streaked by, shrieking and swerving in unison, their fine streaming tail plumes enhancing their speed. Round and round they circled, selecting mates on the wing, and dipping close to the cliff face in search of fissures and cavities suitable for nesting. From time to time a frigate bird, black, slender and as swift as the wind itself, would plummet into their midst from its soaring position high above. The tropic birds would instantly disperse back out to the safety of the unbroken sea, but rarely before the pirating frigate had

succeeded in intercepting one of them in masterful midair assault, upending its hapless victim by a wingtip or tail feather and inducing it to relinquish the day's fish catch from its crop.

As the sinking sun turned to scarlet, more and more albatrosses dropped down onto the plateau inland from the cliff edge, a dangerous manoeuvre ranging at best from a barely controlled crash landing to a sometimes fatal tangle with the unyielding thorny vegetation. Once on the ground, however, they soon regained their stateliness, walking away with a rhythmic sway in search of hungry chicks secluded in the dense scrub. The waved albatross is unique in that it does not build any sort of nest, but hatches its single egg, rolling it freely along the ground during the two months' incubation. The chick, a waddling mocha-coloured fluff ball, wanders off alone in search of shade to escape the day's noontime heat while its parents are away feeding.

As daylight began to fade, familiar moaning, trumpeting and clapping sounds rose from small clearings screened by vegetation, heralding one of the most enthralling natural ballets to be seen anywhere in Galapagos, or indeed in the world. Facing off in twos and threes, unmated albatrosses would engage in a superbly choreographed courtship display sequence. In

Masked boobies fish the waters between islands, often following feeding dolphins, Daphne.

Boobies are extraordinary divers, aligning their wings in a perfectly streamlined arrow shape, Floreana.

breathtakingly strict cadence and order of progression, combining bowing, yawning, sky pointing, cooing, preening and bill fencing, they seek out subtle affinities of character and establish mutual trust, eventually leading to lifelong pair bonds. Throughout virtually the entire nesting season from April to December, at the end of each day single birds up to five years old come together to dance, while paired adults join in at the end of the season as they prepare to head out for three or four months of solitary wanderings.

Meanwhile, in the gathering twilight, another ethereal spectacle was taking place along the cliff edge, where flocks of elegant swallow-tailed gulls were lifting off like delicate white wisps against the thickening dusk, their thin screams whisked away by the wind as they headed off into the sunset on nightly feeding forays far out to sea. They would return by dawn to feed their single chicks in pebble-lined nests on narrow cliff ledges, in truly un-gull-like fashion. With pink feet and huge red-rimmed eyes adapted for night vision, this stunningly beautiful bird shares the status of the waved albatross as a Galapagos endemic species (although again a few stray pairs may reach as far north as tiny Malpelo Rock off the coast of Colombia).

Less specific in their oceanic feeding range than the albatross, swallow-tailed gulls inhabit most islands in Galapagos, as do several other seabirds nesting on Española Island. Crowding the island's eastern and western tips are sizeable colonies of both masked and blue-footed boobies, expert high divers each specializing in their own fish prey and feeding environment, yet sharing amazing adaptations in plunge diving prowess. Blue-foots are coastal feeders, incredibly agile at diving at high speed into tight spaces and near-shore shallows, while masked boobies are heavy birds that search the open waters between islands, pursuing passing schools of sardines and mackerel, spending most of their time in association with feeding schools of dolphins. Plummeting from great heights, both birds can accelerate to speeds of up to 100 kilometres per hour before they enter the water like a streamlined arrow, chasing fish ten metres or more below the surface.

In the raucous nesting colony boobies are a delight to watch, especially the blue-foot whose courting dance rivals that of the albatross in elaborate gestures of symbolic significance. Everything the bird does in this process is deliberate and exaggerated, from cocky strutting to make-believe placement of nesting material that is designed purely for show, in no way serving to build a nest. The enthralling display begins with a gaudy, feet-

to-the-fore landing salute, and escalates through many self-important bows and nods to a rocking dance, the bird slowly lifting each fully-spread blue web. The whole performance culminates in an all out sky pointing contortion, with wings, beak and tail all straining vertically at the same time. For full effect this startling act is accompanied by a drawn-out whistle if the actor is a male, or an equally plaintive honk for the female's turn.

Bold, loud and endlessly animated, blue-footed boobies generate in me a constant source of fascination, as they do in all visitors, no matter how many hundreds of hours I have watched them before. The colour of their feet, as intense as the brightest old-fashioned skin-diving flippers they seem to have inspired, represent those rare synthetic hues one would never expect to find in nature. And yet, as if to suggest that anything is possible, at the north-eastern edge of the archipelago the blue-foot is replaced by its cousin, the red-footed booby, every bit as dazzling in its choice of footwear.

Genovesa Island, like Española, is the gathering point for seabirds from another vast tract of unbroken ocean. Where Española is the first land encountered by birds coming from the south-east, Genovesa represents the primary landfall for a north-easterly approach, attracting species whose lives are driven by the availability of tropical flying fish common in the warm, low-salinity, nutrient-poor waters between Galapagos and Panama. There is no better expert in this field than the red-footed booby, slender and lithe, capable of chasing and capturing darting fish in mid-air pursuit.

Just like Española, Genovesa is also an extremely arid island, its low-lying plateaux licked by salt mist during most of the year. Rains are limited to a few downpours in a good year, or sometimes none at all for several years running. Still, its rusty-coloured, clinkered lavas are well cloaked in a dwarf forest of silvery *palo santo* trees that stretches over virtually the entire island, right to the sheer brim of its twin calderas.

Like so many islands in the Galapagos, Genovesa is a little world unto itself, one which gives me a rush of excitement each and every time I spot its unprepossessing outline appear on the distant horizon. Contrary to its English name, Tower Island, Genovesa is a flat island rising a mere 60 metres above sea level. Powerful east-west currents in this region frequently deflect the course of slow-moving small boats, to the extent that from time

Blue-footed boobies nest throughout the islands, Tagus Cove, Isabela.

Red-footed boobies court and nest in trees on the outer islands, especially the northern ones, Wolf.

61

Storm petrels flutter low over the water, pattering with their feet as they feed.

entrance, Darwin Bay is completely surrounded by cliffs, black, grey and reddish lava layers painted in variegated guano hues, with the authors of this natural graffiti everywhere in evidence. There is an incessant commotion in the air. Storm petrels increase to swarming proportions over the seaward cliff edge, like crazed moths around a lantern, tens of thousands of the tiny birds jostling for nesting space under the crusty lava. Flashing white against the dark cliffs, tropic birds streak past while swallow-tailed gulls parachute slowly from ledge to ledge. Dark and unobtrusive, noddies and shearwaters circle low over the tranquil water, while booby and frigate traffic above is constant. Indeed frigates rise in tight columns, gyrating slowly higher and higher as they ride the thermal updrafts the morning sun generates over the island. Never moving a feather, they climb ever higher until wending their way in and out of tufty clouds.

At the bottom of the bay a tiny, white, coral beach against the cliff base guards a set of tidal pools where sedentary endemic lava gulls live. Here are sandy flats covered in green salt bush and lush clumps of mangroves. Red-footed boobies flock to this more tender vegetation for the purpose of collecting twigs to take back to their nests inland. The entire island is evenly dotted with a huge population of red-footed boobies, numbering an estimated 140,000 pairs, probably the largest colony in the world. Far more nimble than the masked and blue-footed boobies, red-foots are at ease in trees, building sturdy twig nests to raise their single chick. With the exception of a small proportion of white birds, the usually creamy-brown red-foots blend well into the leafless landscape, yet their brilliant red feet, when backlit by the slanting rays of the late afternoon sun, can glow almost as brightly as a ship's port side lantern.

If red-footed boobies are the most numerous birds on Genovesa, the frigates are even more conspicuous, due to their size and their habit of concentrating their nesting activities near the shore. Two species are present, the vast majority being the pelagic, flying fish dependent, greater frigates, intermingled with small numbers of the slightly larger magnificent frigates. The latter's scavenging feeding habits make it a coastal species, therefore more commonly seen in the central islands.

Befitting birds of the warmer tropics, the greatest level of nesting activity is reached towards the end of our warmest months, around March and

to time one will pass right on by, never coming within sight of the island. Yet long before it materializes, the determined flight paths of boobies and frigates commuting to and from their nests is often the best indicator of the heading the helmsman should follow.

As the thin, blue-black line of land defines itself on the horizon the bird traffic soon increases exponentially. Storm petrels flutter low over the waves like butterflies, red-footed boobies zigzag into the troughs after the occasional silver glint of a flying fish, small flocks of fast-travelling masked boobies head purposefully toward their nesting colony, and frigates, slender, near motionless silhouettes, ride almost weightless, high on the sea wind.

Sails straining, the small yacht shoots for the gap in the jagged black cliffs reaching out like arms to either side of the pass that leads into Darwin Bay, an old submerged volcanic caldera breached only on its southern side. Slipping through this entrance you pass from the current-tossed sea outside to the sudden calm of windless, sheltered waters within, and at once the cacophony of seabird sounds invades from all sides. Except for its narrow

Previous page: The beautifully choreographed courtship of the waved albatross is a mesmerizing spectacle, Española.

A new pair of greater frigates spends time becoming acquainted before the male's pouch deflates, Genovesa.

April, when the frigates are in the full flurry of mate selection, a process centred on the males' astounding air-filled scarlet balloons, or gular sacks, which they develop for the occasion. Everywhere small groups of males huddle in the low bushes, occupying potential nesting sites. Each time an eligible female swoops overhead they erupt into a frenzy of collective attention grabbing, throwing their heads back to reveal the outlandish size of their red balloons, cooing and fluttering their two metre-plus wings for added effect. Females are choosy and many days may pass before one will descend and accept a mate after closer examination. Undaunted, each male may sit for two or three weeks without a break, endlessly repeating the performance, and moving on to a new site if his more successful neighbours begin nest building with new-found mates. The spectacle reaches a crescendo morning and evening, when the heat of the sun is less overpowering, while in the meantime hundreds of red-footed boobies prune down the shrubs all around in their constant quest for nesting material. Their harsh screams echo almost continuously around the caldera, as no sooner do they take off with a branch that some passing male frigate, also engaged in nest building, closes in for some lightning-fast, mid-air thievery. A single desirable twig may change beaks a dozen times before coming to rest in a nest far from where it was first plucked.

The vibrant pace of life hardly lets up on Genovesa, though in the cooler season, when fluffy chicks sit alone on their nests while parents are away plying the warmer waters far to the north in search of food, things may look sleepy by comparison. It thus comes as a striking contrast to look westward to the next two islands, Marchena and Pinta. Here the breeze blows silently past sentry-like cacti, around volcanic cones, and over barren black lava flows. Barely a handful of swallow-tailed gulls can be found here, demonstrating emphatically that there is no value in a second-best choice for seabirds seeking land nearest to their ocean haunts. Just as the geographical distribution of the seabirds follows clear and simple patterns dictated by the surrounding seas, other Galapagos animals each have their own set of factors that determine where each one may thrive. Pinta and Marchena, for example, each harbour a separate species of endemic lava lizard, whose ancestors were cast ashore by the vagaries of ocean drift. Genovesa, on the other hand, has never been colonized by any land reptile

Red-footed boobies gathering nest material near the beach often fall prey to thieving frigates, Genovesa.

The colourful display of male frigates trying to impress soaring females decorates Darwin Bay, Genovesa.

at all, whereas Pinta, alone among these three northern islands, gave rise to its own, unique subspecies of saddleback tortoise.

Just like many of the seabirds, however, Galapagos pinnipeds — the fur seals and sea lions — are also found in colonies whose locations reflect easy access to favourite feeding grounds, although in many cases these lie between islands rather than in offshore waters. Both fur seals and sea lions are found in good numbers on Genovesa, the former scattered in cool caves and shady fissures at the cliff base, the latter concentrated for the most part on an exposed beach along the south shore. To become truly acquainted with the enthralling lives of the gregarious sea lions, however, one must travel back amongst the central islands, from the boulder shores of Plazas to the turquoise shallows of Santa Fe.

Male frigates may take two weeks or more to attract a mate for the year-long nesting cycle, Genovesa.

Blue-footed Booby Dance

Performed in dense and noisy colonies, everything about the booby's courtship is deliberate and designed to emphasize coordination between the pair. The male whistles and the female honks as they sky-point in turn (centre top), strut and present each other with ceremonial nesting material (centre, bottom) even though they build no nest. Every so often one will fly off and return with a proud salute of blue feet thrust forward just before landing (below). All this will help the pair work closely together to raise their chicks (far right), duties they share equally.

A sea lion cow relaxes in the cool spray of a nearby blowhole, Punta Suarez, Española.

4 SURFLINE MEDLEY
Sea Lions at Play

Many of my earliest childhood memories are laced with the presence of sea lions. Unlike encounters with the far-ranging seabirds of the outlying islands, those with sea lions were frequent without the need to travel far from home. Yet, as is so often the case with the changing perspective of acquired years, my response to these engaging animals changed dramatically as I became better acquainted with them, as indeed did their attitude towards humans. As far back as I can recall, many a grey dawn was greeted with the distant bark of a territorial bull guarding his handful of females on a tiny islet a mile away from our house, a haunting, monotonous sound carried on the brisk sea wind. These were the days before motorized traffic in Academy Bay, when barely 600 to 800 people lived here and only a handful of dugout canoes or tiny dinghies were paddled to favourite fishing spots. When we did encounter sea lions, unaccustomed to seeing people as they were, they seemed nervous and unpredictable, driven by a mixture of curiosity and fear, which was only a reflection of our own uncertainties in the presence of a large, agile, intelligent, territorial wild animal. When boat traffic increased around the harbour, these few sea lions simply relocated to a more secluded island further offshore. The days of deep mutual trust, the amazing inter-species rapport that today is one of the hallmarks of Galapagos experiences, expressed as much by the rambunctious playfulness of pups as by the beachmasters' studious disregard for human swimmers, was still years away.

Play-fighting young bulls must spend years honing their ability to defend a territory, Punta Espinosa, Fernandina.

In 1964, with our tiny boat the *Puck* proving seaworthy and reliable, we made our first trip to Santa Fe Island, only 35 kilometres east of our home. For years we had watched the play of light each day caress the high ochre and grey cliffs in the distance, as the afternoon sun bypassed the ever-present *garua* clouds over Santa Cruz and painted fleeting colours on the face of Santa Fe. Now, approaching for the first time, those sere cliffs came to life. As we skirted around the island we spotted our first ever Galapagos hawk, soaring high above the headland. Reaching the turquoise waters of the only anchorage on the far side, we were at once surrounded, even besieged, by sea lions. From all directions they came: pups leaping and somersaulting and egging each other on in tight groups; large bulls looking stern, circling our small hull, growling and rolling their eyes as they do when meaning to intimidate a rival. When we landed gingerly on the idyllic white beach, the entire mass of sea lions asleep on the sand rushed into the sea in a sudden stampede, so surprised were they to find humans in their midst. From the comforting safety of the shallows their

Pups cavort endlessly in the clear shallows near the colony, Santa Fe.

At nightfall arguments over choice sleeping spots are frequent, Rabida.

After playing in the shallows, pups like to roll in the clean beach sands, Mosquera.

fear soon turned to curiosity and, emboldened by numbers, the entire mob followed our every move with obvious interest. The beachmaster bulls, however, were not amused by all the commotion, charging us repeatedly up the beach with bluster and bravado designed for maximum intimidation. When we departed, our rowing skiff was followed across the bay by a long string of tussling, snorting, sinuous bodies jostling for better views. Curiosity, apprehension and fascination translated into great excitement, feelings that amazingly were shared in equal measure by the clustered pinnipeds and our own little family, clinging, white-knuckled, to the rocking gunnels of our dinghy. That night we set up our tent in the only flat area we could find on a small islet sheltering the bay, unaware that this was also the sleeping spot for most of the bachelor bulls hanging around the outskirts of the colony. No sooner had we gone to sleep than a violent coughing fit erupted just outside the tent door, followed by deep throaty snoring. Until sunrise our exit was securely blocked by jostling, heaving, brown bodies.

More than 30 years have passed now and I look back with amusement to those days of wonder and caution. Many things have remained the same on this small island: the turquoise waters and sparkling beaches, the grey-brown cliffs and the soaring hawks; and the noisy, gregarious sea lions are still in residence. Now, as then, humans and sea lions remain fascinated with each other, both species being curious by nature. But today a new level of comfort has been reached in the relationship.

Hardly a day in the year now passes without at least one, and usually a number, of boats bobbing at anchor in Santa Fe, off-loading group after group of camera-toting visitors. On the same beach where sea lions once panicked at our very appearance, people now spread their beach towels within arm's reach of newborn pups nursing contentedly, the rotund cows barely casting an indifferent glance at their human neighbours. The beachmaster bulls guarding their breeding rights chase away rivals while ignoring splashing human swimmers. Yet for the gaggles of adolescent pups, whose sole purpose in life is to play, the excitement and entertainment value of the human presence never wears off. Their long-forgotten fears have simply been replaced with an endless succession of daring tricks and innovative games as often as not clearly intended to bring about a response in the observer.

There is nothing the young sea lions seem to enjoy more than to be joined in their own underwater realm where they are both coy and cocky. They twist and turn, somersault and pirouette. They streak away in a cloud

A mother and her newborn pup recognize each other's voice amid hundreds of others, Cape Douglas, Fernandina.

of bubbles and return with a flirtatious twirl. Their world is weightless, their intelligence vibrant. Above all, their urge to play is possessed with fiery energy. Their every move speaks of uninhibited exuberance, of the most natural expression of joy. When visiting the realm of the sea lion pup, never has the human observer, whether snorkeller or diver, felt so uplifted — and at once so hopelessly awkward and ungainly. Perhaps what touches us most is this lithe young mammal's overwhelming urge to demonstrate his extraordinary abilities, his obvious desire to *show us* what he can do. For an instant he hangs upside down, deliberately blowing large bubbles, then spins and catches them before they reach the surface. In a group, the boisterous pups retrieve sea stars or sea shells and steal them from each other. Soon we, as mere humans, are reduced to spluttering unco-ordination, yet our ecstasy seems to soar to unknown heights. Grinning, we squeak and giggle through flooded snorkels, flail and roll until, ears and nose filled with water, we rise for uncertain breath. As anyone who has

Highly manoeuvrable under water, a pup scatters a school of black striped salemas, Seymour.

Sea Lion Games

As sea lions grow up their urge to play knows no bounds, especially when they are still nourished by their mother's milk. On land and under water they spend endless hours cavorting, bulls-to-be tussling and play fighting (below), or just spinning and chasing each other with infinite agility, as in this sea grotto in James Bay (far right). One of their favourite pastimes is body surfing where the waves build offshore, riding just inside the teetering crests of the breakers (right & lower right) or somersaulting above to catch a breath (upper right) before returning to the starting point.

Young iguanas too small to resist cold waters feed on algae-covered, exposed rocks, Academy Bay, Santa Cruz.

in weight), begin to swim out to sea. Heads held just above the water, their legs trailing close along their bodies, they undulate from side to side with a snake-like motion, using their long, vertically flattened tails to propel themselves at a modest cruising speed rarely exceeding 1.6 kilometres per hour. Doggedly they swim against the onrushing breakers, eventually reaching offshore areas which they know from experience to be the site of submerged shallow reefs where their favourite seaweed grows lushly. One by one they disappear, diving down some five to ten metres to the bottom to graze on the seafloor, sharing their undersea pastures with sea turtles and large schools of reef fish.

Marine iguanas are capable of remaining submerged for an hour or more, but their dives rarely last longer than five or ten minutes between surfacing for breath. It is not oxygen supply that limits their feeding time, but rather the loss of body heat to the cool waters, which at times may drop well below 15°C. As they feed they are losing heat fast, and the

With the ebbing tide iguanas stream down to feed along with sally-lightfoot crabs, Punta Espinosa, Fernandina.

A breeding male takes a quick break from guarding his territory to feed in a tide pool. Punta Suarez, Española.

colder they get the more difficult it is for them to remain alert and active. Like many marine animals, they are capable of dramatically reducing both their heart rate and the flow of blood to any but the most vital organs, all in an effort to conserve body heat. Even so, after about an hour the reptiles are becoming dangerously chilled. Their movements become sluggish and it is time for them to return to shore. Laboriously they fight the current and the slop of the waves. Again and again, the swells toss them brutally against the rocks, only to pull them away just as they struggle to establish a foothold. At last their sharp claws catch hold of a fissure or barnacle and they drag themselves ashore, sometimes so exhausted they can barely move. Indeed, at times of exceptionally high seas and strong, cold currents I have seen dozens of full-grown iguanas drifting far out to sea, quite alive but unable to move from hypothermia, doomed to a certain death unless washed naturally back to shore. Sailing between Isabela and Fernandina I

Large males swim out into deeper waters to graze the sea floor amid yellowtail surgeonfish, Cape Douglas, Fernandina.

Overleaf: *Marine iguanas basking by the thousands, Punta Espinosa, Fernandina.*

81

Cool currents bathe the iguana's realm in morning fog, shared here with a lava heron, Cape Douglas, Fernandina.

many large stringy clumps streaming in the foam. In the best feeding areas the intense grazing pressure keeps the fast-growing algae, which can increase in weight six-fold every two weeks, cropped so closely it forms a layer barely one or two millimetres thick.

Each day the iguanas' feeding procession takes place at a different time, as the reptiles are somehow intimately attuned to the shifting cycle of the tides. Unhampered by continental shelves and other obstructing land masses, in Galapagos the low tide invariably falls close to two and a half hours after both moonrise and moonset. And as the moon's orbit takes approximately fifty minutes longer than the solar day to complete, the twice daily tides fall correspondingly later each time. It is a mystery that has intrigued me all my life, and which eludes me to this day, how the humble iguana unfailingly senses the approach of the ebbing tide, even when well out of sight of the wave wash. Is it smell, the changing pitch of the wave action, or an internal clock that guides them?

The iguanas' feeding forays always seem hurried, bordering on frantic for an animal that spends most of its life doing nothing. With the turning tide the iguanas return to dry land in droves. As they reach the warm rocks they stop to sprawl on the black slabs. Spread-eagled, with the sun on their backs and their stomachs pressed against the superheated ground, they soak in all the warmth they can. Their first priority now is to regain lost heat. On a sunny day it takes most iguanas only an hour or two to fully warm up, piled together congenially on their favourite basking rocks. Ironically, at this point, they are once again in danger of losing control of their internal temperature, a problem they solve by what is known scientifically as 'behavioural thermoregulation'. They simply turn and face into the sun, raising their bodies slightly to allow air flow beneath them and presenting only their snouts to the scorching rays. Thus, by shifting the orientation and angle of their bodies and varying the surface area exposed to both sun and hot substrate, they can successfully absorb or shed heat at will.

The ideal body temperature range for an iguana to be able to function efficiently is surprisingly narrow, virtually the same as our own, with only two or three degrees tolerance. Until this is reached simple biological functions, such as digestion, cannot resume, yet should it rise above about 45°C they would quickly overheat and die. They must therefore strike a

Clinging to tideline rocks with sharp claws, females are oblivious to pounding waves, Academy Bay, Santa Cruz.

once picked up a dozen of these castaways several miles out to sea and piled their rigid bodies in our cockpit. Within half an hour of lying in the sun they perked up and scrambled across the decks, none the worse for wear. Paradoxically, the cold currents that nurture their abundant food supplies are also the greatest threat to these animals that depend upon their environment to govern their body temperature.

For the smaller iguanas, from hatchlings to mature females over half a metre long, the dangers of rapid heat loss outweigh the benefits of lush feeding grounds offshore. As a result they rarely venture beyond the exposed foreshore at low tide, where they face the brunt of the pounding surf instead. Alert and eager, they scamper about here and there, clinging tenaciously to the rocks with their specially adapted curving claws. With quick jerking movements they tip their blunt snouts to one side or the other, using tiny rasp-like, three-cusped teeth to scrape the near-invisible algae growth from the wave-worn rocks. What seems like random munching is in fact selective nibbling, entire mouthfuls being spat out if the wrong seaweed is inadvertently taken. Methodically they select the tender, most digestible red and green forms, shunning the coarser brown types and ignoring the

A Galapagos hawk can make an easy kill when nesting females have no rocks to cling to, Cape Hammond, Fernandina.

Breaking through the tough skin with difficulty, a juvenile hawk feeds on his parent's kill, Cape Hammond, Fernandina.

balance between the rigours of making daily feeding trips into the frigid sea and surviving on barren, mostly shadeless lava shores where the searing ground can be too hot for a person to stand on.

Come night-time, when temperatures drop abruptly, iguanas will pool their collective warmth until morning by gathering together in snug, though untidy, piles. It is this ability to control their body temperature by altering their behaviour rather than by requiring shelter, that sets the marine iguanas apart from all other reptiles. In addition, the salt-secreting glands in their foreheads that act somewhat like a second set of kidneys, have been perfected far beyond those of any other species, even though these organs are shared by many other reptiles and seabirds. In the iguanas this mechanism is so efficient they can eliminate salt from their bloodstream in concentrations almost twice as high as seawater, a crucial factor considering the environment in which they live.

Common on all the islands, the total marine iguana population for the

A sally-lightfoot crab carefully picks skin debris from a colourful breeding male, Punta Suarez, Española.

archipelago has been estimated at between 200,000 and 300,000, although numbers undoubtedly fluctuate according to pressures from feral animals in some places as well as the vagaries of climatic conditions. Amazingly for an animal that depends on the sea for survival, the powerful cold currents that flow between islands have proven enough of a barrier that distinct races have developed in isolation on various islands. On Genovesa, marine iguanas are small and slender and never reach more than 1.6 kilograms, whereas on Isabela, massive males over ten times that bulk are the norm. Those of Española Island acquire brilliantly coloured patterns with gaudy patches of bright red and copper-oxide green during the breeding season, especially the large males, while several other island races show more subtle size and colour variations.

In spite of their adaptations, marine iguanas are also quite capable of taking advantage of new opportunities. On Seymour Island for some years they have taken to grazing the beach plant, *Batis maritima*, and when a dead fish or fresh sea lion placenta presents itself they are quick to cash in on the protein-rich meal. Trusting by nature, they even make themselves at home on the busy village piers and hotel fronts in Academy Bay, ignoring

the bustle of modern day Galapagos humanity and even accepting scraps of food.

Along the south cliffs of Santa Fe one hot, sunny afternoon I dropped in with some friends on a team of scientists conducting a long-term study of marine iguana population dynamics. Their camp was accessible only via a hair-raising landing on a steep jumble of slippery boulders relentlessly pounded by the sea, and aptly dubbed 'Miedo', Spanish for 'Fright'. Under the scant shade of a sun-tattered tarpaulin, the head scientist, who rarely saw visitors, graciously offered tea and snacks all round, and in no time we were engrossed in conversation. Cup and biscuit in hand, what I had not noticed was the other camp resident: a hefty, pale-yellow, land iguana, cousin of the marine type, who had taken great interest in the opening of a rusty tin box in which all camp food was kept. Suddenly I was rammed by a charging miniature dinosaur and, as I looked around dumbfounded, realized the biscuit had disappeared from my hand. The fat lizard, his benevolent, built-in, reptilian grin more noticeable than ever, sat munching nearby.

Later in the day, more by luck than skill, we made it back into our boat without a dunking. I turned to look back at the surf-beaten foreshore, and there, seen intermittently through curtains of white froth, black dragons clung oblivious to the sea's fury, munching peacefully. As we motored away I felt a wave of affection for these adaptable and resourceful though primitive beasts, terrestrial or marine, who can recognize a good thing when they see it, whether tender seaweed or sweet biscuit.

Along the wild lava shores of Fernandina, where cold upwellings ensure abundant supplies of algal growth, they thrive in densities surpassing a staggering 3,000 iguanas per kilometre of coast. This is marine iguana heaven, where life is pared down to the most elemental. There are no introduced carnivores here, only a few natural predators such as snakes and herons taking a proportion of each year's hatchlings, plus some Galapagos hawks occasionally killing a few adult females, especially when they are exposed on sand patches, busy digging their nesting burrows. In their dragon-like forms there is great beauty, one that I have spent many years trying to capture on film.

To ward off the night's dropping temperature, marine iguanas pile together, Cape Douglas, Fernandina.

Great blue herons are consummate stalkers of tiny hatchlings, Punta Espinosa, Fernandina.

Nesting

For a couple of weeks each year at the height of the warm season all gravid marine iguana females gather in small pockets of sand just above the tideline to nest (upper, near right). They dig slanting burrows and deposit, on average, only two eggs each before filling in the nest and levelling the sand over it. For the eggs to hatch, incubated by the warmth of the sun, the right humidity level must be found in the sand, the females milling about and digging many test pits. With so many iguanas and so little space, fighting is almost constant, especially between those guarding recently completed nests and others still searching for the perfect spot (middle and far right). Though rarely biting and causing no serious harm, the protracted struggles consist of wrestling, shoving and ramming heads, until exhaustion determines the outcome (sequence below).

A lava flow pouring into the sea attracts hundreds of seabirds to the bonanza of dead fish, Cape Hammond, Fernandina.

6 COLD SEAS AND BURNING ROCKS
The Western Fringe of Life

To travel from centrally located Santa Cruz to the shores of the westernmost islands is truly like a journey through time. On the map, 140 kilometre-long Isabela Island looks like a gigantic sea-horse curled protectively around an enormous egg, Fernandina. The air is clear and cool here, the seas often calm and windless. The cloud layers are high and sparse, giving rise to some of the most spectacular sunsets in Galapagos. In all directions one is surrounded by the massive, steep-sided, symmetrical domes of young shield volcanoes. Five of these enormous geologic structures make up the length of Isabela Island, from south to north: Cerro Azul, Sierra Negra, Alcedo, Darwin and Wolf, the latter rising to a height of 1,700 metres, the highest point in Galapagos. Volcan Ecuador, the remnants

of a sixth, much smaller shield, clings precariously to the north-western tip of the island, the sea-horse's mouth, deeply breached and down-faulted mysteriously into the sea, like the broken throne of some departed volcano spirit. Across the narrow Bolivar Channel separating the two islands, the lone volcano of Fernandina guards six thousand kilometres of unbroken Pacific Ocean to the west. Like sentries feigning sleep but ready to spring into action at any moment, these volcanoes are truly very much alive, the epicentre of on-going volcanic growth springing up from the depth of the Galapagos hotspot. Their flanks streaked by thousands of overlapping lava flows shimmering in a blue and purple haze, some barely cooled, they take it in turns to redesign the shape of their islands every few years. At such

Sea mist drifts ashore from the cool, rich upwellings of the Cromwell Current, Punta Vicente Roca, Isabela.

times they grumble and spew gasses high into the atmosphere and send rivers of molten lava to extend the contours of their shorelines.

Rounding the north-western tip of Isabela at Cape Berkeley, where the equator runs squarely into the gigantic altar of Volcan Ecuador, is like slipping through a gateway from one realm to another which, ecologically speaking, is indeed the case. Long ocean swells pound the base of towering, dike-riddled cliffs. Jagged fingers of slag-like lava spawn wisps of mist and fog where the sun-baked land is assaulted by frigid waters from the abyss. Here at the interface between the untamed ocean and the fierce, ungiving land lies a thriving ecosystem, a fringe of life whose existence is held in balance by the bounty of the sea and the solidity of the land. Sedentary flightless cormorants and Galapagos penguins fish the coastal waters, while fur seals and sea lions venture further out to sea after squid and schooling fish. Marine iguanas divide their time between grazing shallow reefs and basking on the sunbaked lava shore in congenial multitudes. Blue-footed

A juvenile pelican roosts on a day-old lava flow as a new lava headland is formed, Cape Douglas, Fernandina.

93

Galapagos penguins are found only where upwellings nurture abundant inshore life, Bartolome.

boobies gather offshore in reeling flocks, pelting the sea like hail, returning to shore to nest in equally crowded gatherings on the slopes of naked tuff cones. All this diversity of life shares its dependency on the sea for feeding and on the land for breeding.

The dynamo that drives this unique community is the strange phenomenon of the Cromwell Current, a deep flow of oceanic waters drawing its origins from the distant western Pacific. This current, also known as the Equatorial Countercurrent, runs far beneath the equator in the opposite direction to the vast westward movement of the surface waters forming the South Equatorial Current that predominates in Galapagos. Thus, originating in the far Indo-Pacific and travelling eastward along the equator, the Cromwell Current runs along the cold, dark depths of the sea for thousands of kilometres, gathering stores of nutrients from the organic debris raining down from the sunlit layers above. Only when these waters encounter the massive bulk of the Galapagos Platform are they forced upward, welling to the surface around the shores of Fernandina and Isabela.

Blue-footed boobies rain from the sky on a fish school pursued by dolphins and tuna, Punta Mangle, Fernandina.

Having finished feeding, a large male iguana rises to the surface among schooling dusky chubs, Cape Douglas, Fernandina.

My first foray into these wondrous waters was in 1968, the most adventurous by far of our travels on the *Kim*, when we sailed for three weeks in the shadow of the brooding volcanoes. As children, I recall scrambling with my brother among labyrinthine lava valleys and ridges, climbing high through giant mangrove forests where the rare tool-using mangrove finch sang, and searching for flame-coloured scallop shells in a wonderland of sun-bleached coral heads lifted out of the sea by volcanic action some years previously. Since those early days I have returned dozens of times, in derelict fishing boats and in luxury tour ships, hiking, camping and diving, or exploring every nook and cranny of the western shores in a small dinghy. Strange and surprising contrasts come hard and fast here: flamingos and pintails feeding in small freshwater pools surrounded by kilometre after kilometre of lifeless lava fields, green turtles mating among squadrons of golden rays in clear mangrove lagoons, and penguins calling like miniature foghorns through the misty dawn as they head out from their lava nesting caves into the dull greyish-green sea. On scorching days

The land is bare while the coastal shallows of Fernandina team with life, such as feeding marine iguanas, Punta Espinosa.

Life or death moments on the Fernandina shore: bull sea lions locked in serious combat ...

... and flightless cormorants, mother and chick, warding off a hungry but inexperienced young hawk, both Cape Douglas.

I have assisted vulcanologists meticulously measuring the tilt of the land that might herald a new eruption from Fernandina's restless volcano, and helped a team of National Park wardens in the unsavoury task of exterminating feral dogs that for years decimated the native wildlife of Isabela.

Fernandina and Isabela could not be more different in this regard: the former is easily the largest island in the world (outside polar regions) to have had virtually no impact from mankind to alter its pristine balance, while the latter, being the largest in the Galapagos, has become host to virtually every imaginable type of domestic animal gone wild. For Fernandina the human onslaught has come in its marine environment, first lobsters and sharks, then a most unlikely creature sought-after in oriental cuisine: the lowly sea cucumber, setting the scene for a 'gold rush' of devastating proportions in recent years.

To this day, however, Fernandina's spell is not broken. At Cape Douglas on the north-western tip, is a tiny cove offering protection from the onslaught of the ocean swells, a miniature haven for the young of many species, whose parents ply the nearby waters for a living. Here I have lived for weeks with no shelter and no reminders of modern life beyond camera and snorkelling gear, sensing the rhythm by which the native animals live, breed and die in harmony with their environment. Vignettes from these experiences have taught me to understand the timeless nature of a classic Galapagos day.

As I slept under Fernandina's stars, rice rats scrabbled in my hair, cute plump rodents not much bigger than mice and as curious and unafraid as any Galapagos creature. In the moonlight, pairs of courting penguins shuffled up the beach searching the lava fringe for unoccupied nesting caves, past sea lion pups suckling noisily from their mothers' retractable nipples. At dawn the island lay cloaked in cool, still fog, while busy flightless cormorants carried clumps of seaweed to their nests along the wave wash. With the morning sun burning away the mist, marine iguanas stirred from their entwined throngs, heading for a seaweed meal at low tide. Two neighbouring bull sea lions, unable to resolve their differences by ritualized posturing, suddenly engaged in furious combat which eventually tinted

Mother fur seals head out at sunset to feed on deep water squid, leaving young pups behind, Cape Douglas, Fernandina.

A few kilometres in from the shore, the land is renewed as lava spews from the volcano's flank, Fernandina.

Fountaining lava accompanies escaping gases as new spatter cones build amid a scorched palo santo forest.

the tide pool they had shared with their wasted blood. As the afternoon cooled a family of Galapagos hawks, two males and one female — a rare case of polyandric mating — brought their fledgling chick to experiment with subduing prey, eventually dispatching a hapless marine iguana. In the fading dusk, mother fur seals headed out on their nightly squid hunt, leaving behind wide-eyed pups, their lonely cries resembling those of human infants. The brief splash of sunset colours sometimes brought a flurry of exuberant leaps from a group of bottlenose dolphins near shore, while further out a feeding Bryde's whale's blow ignited like fire. In the chilly twilight of the gathering dusk a young sea lion cow gave birth for the first time, sally-lightfoot crabs moving in to carry away the placenta. Another night fell over the Fernandina shore, and with it the cycle was completed yet again. One more magical day had passed in a natural paradise as yet neither found nor lost, but simply unharried, at peace with time.

Yet stability is a relative concept in the scheme of nature and evolutionary processes. Nowhere is this better illustrated than on the virgin shores of Fernandina. Early in 1995 I was away from Galapagos when the island started to erupt. A spectacular fissure had opened on the western flank, with profuse lava flows pouring into the sea. When my mother tracked me down with the news, thinking I would not want to miss this event, my response was a resigned 'No chance'. While living in Academy Bay, half a dozen times over the years I had dropped everything I was doing at the first news of an eruption, hopped aboard the trusty *Inti*, and headed west in hopes of recording the spectacle. But catching a Fernandina eruption had proven as elusive as chasing shooting stars, so brief and unpredictable was the activity, often dying down within hours. This time I was over 10,000 kilometres away in New Zealand.

Four days later, however, I stood on Fernandina's rugged western coast, only 20 kilometres south of Cape Douglas, staring in awe at one of the most formidable scenes nature has to offer. The entire side of the island appeared as if on fire. Under a heavy pall of amber fumes, braided rivers of molten lava snaked down some five kilometres from the spurting, fountaining vents to the shore, wending their way in and out of small patches of vegetation and blanketing the land in smouldering rubble. For

Flowing faster than water, a river of fluid basalt bursts its banks as it contours a tree-covered hill.

A vast lava flow illuminates the night sky with its eerie glow as it pushes forth towards the sea, February 1995.

Uncomprehending wildlife fail to heed the destructive advance of the new lava: courting flightless cormorants, ...

eight mesmerizing days I lived under the spell of the volcano, trying to comprehend the evolutionary significance of this Dantesque event, no doubt replayed thousands of times since the birth of the island.

Under the mantle of dusk I sat not ten metres from the edge of the flowing lava, listening to the hellish crackle, hiss and roar as it plunged into boiling seas amid billows of purplish-red steam. In a moonlike landscape I unfurled my bedroll under the eerie glow permeating the heavens, and combed the spicules of barely cooled, airborne scoria from my hair in the morning. I explored the fringes of a ghost forest scalded, charred and wrenched by new volcanic spatter, and sat entranced late one night watching trees flare up where streams of glaring hot lava rushed forth at cataract speeds, until the heat on my face caused me to retreat.

The most bizarre, and unsettling, aspect of the entire experience was to observe the inability of the wildlife to comprehend the destructive powers of the awakened volcano as it temporarily upset the ecological balance of the area. Desperately over-heating marine iguanas facing the oncoming flow, incapable of understanding the source of their distress, clambered in panic onto the red-hot slabs only to burst into flames, or plunged to their death into the boiling wave-wash. Frolicking fur seal pups ventured into steaming coastal waters, with horribly burned flippers as a consequence. Penguins sat gasping in the blazing sun, where the air was only marginally cooler than the sea.

Where the ocean currents swept along the heated coastline, dead marine iguanas washed ashore, while parboiled invertebrates drifted loose and intertidal algae was blanched. Bottom fish rose to the surface everywhere, deprived of oxygen in the tepid layers below. This attracted hundreds of seabirds from all directions that, instead of fleeing the region, converged on the bonanza of dead and dying fish. Pelicans by the score, plus frigate birds, flightless cormorants and even sea lions gorged on parboiled moray eels bobbing in the steaming eddies. For some the feast turned into agony, as pelicans dropped dead on their roosts with burned eyes and pouches, and tiny storm petrels pattered along the surface of the sea with stumpy legs when blistered feet simply dropped off.

Slowly, with the inexorable advance of the fresh lava, a new headland was formed, extending the contours of Fernandina's shoreline several hundred metres westward — just a mile away from Cape Hammond, where

... a fur seal pup who ventured into boiling shallows, with burns to his flippers and eyes...

a small beach and protected tide pool is haven to a remarkable concentration of life similar to the one at Cape Douglas. Here, several dozen young fur seal pups played in sheltered waters while their mothers were at sea, feeding. Hundreds of female marine iguanas were busily engaged in their yearly nesting effort, jostling for space to bury their eggs in the narrow sandy beach. Their frenzied activity allowed a resident family of Galapagos hawks the opportunity of some easy kills.

All the while the volcano was still working relentlessly. Time and again new lava flows began to run down a shallow valley leading toward Cape Hammond, threatening to engulf this oasis of life. I watched apprehensively until they fanned out and stopped. It took several weeks for this eruption to abate, but Cape Hammond was spared. For the time being life continued unaffected. Even today, Fernandina is still redefining its future, and that of all the unique species that make a living on its restless shores.

... a pelican lies dead after feeding on scalded fish —
the price of life around Fernandina's active volcano.

Flightless Cormorants

Flightless cormorants are one of the most extraordinary Galapagos species, numbering well under 2,000 in total and found only in the productive coastal shallows of Isabela and Fernandina. Far from being at a disadvantage through their loss of flight, they have traded this ability for superior diving capabilities. Heavily built, powerful swimmers (below, among dusky chubs), they feed on a large variety of rock bottom fish, extracting octopus from their lairs and even swallowing poison-spined scorpion fish. To aid in diving their feathers trap very little air, becoming waterlogged (far right, top) and thus avoiding buoyancy problems, but obliging them to dry their stunted wings after feeding (near right). Not surprisingly, they are extremely sedentary and spend their entire lives within a very small area of coast, building seaweed-lined nests just above the high tide (centre right). Every time a mate returns from fishing he or she presents the other with a ceremonial nest building gift (far right, bottom), even while raising chicks.

A Galapagos hawk looks on as lava pours from a caldera bench vent into the lake below, August 1978.

7 TO THE BRINK AND BEYOND
Delving into Fernandina's Active Caldera

Shortly before noon on 11 June 1968 Fernandina made history. I will never forget the bright, sunny morning at the end of our warm season, the calm sea, the crystal clear air with hardly a cloud in the sky. We had motored out on the little *Kim* to the deep waters between Santa Cruz and Santa Fe and had just pulled aboard the first dredge haul of rare and delicate sea shell treasures, when someone glanced up and exclaimed 'Look!'. Far to the north-west, rising like a white pillar over the blue horizon, was a cloud unlike any we had seen before. It rose vertically at incredible speed, billowing and contorting, dense and white like whipped cream. My father had long ago imparted his infectious love for watching clouds build and grow. We all knew instantly that this was no ordinary cloud, but rather the

product of some newly awakened volcano, which, by consulting the direction on the chart, we concluded to be Fernandina, 140 kilometres away. What we did not know at that moment was the scope of the eruption, or that its shockwaves would be recorded throughout the western hemisphere.

Within an hour the cloud had lifted off from its base, even though it was still rising. My father brought out his antique sextant and measured its height, later calculated to have reached 20 kilometres. As it grew, it eventually encountered a distinct air layer in the upper atmosphere and began to spread out horizontally like a huge, flat-topped mushroom. By early afternoon its rounded edge had drifted overhead, blocking out the

A hawk lives on the caldera rim, whose floor dropped from 600 to nearly 1,000 metres deep in 1968.

During the 1970s and 1980s, lava flows from peripheral fissures periodically caused the lake to boil.

sun and tinting the daylight with a dull amber tone that told us this was not just water vapour — as it had first appeared — but volcanic ash as well. Before nightfall we returned to port, by which time the air was resonating with unearthly booms every few minutes. Another cloud rose, this one dark and diffuse, its opaque, ash-laden contours expanding quickly, like a gigantic tadpole blocking out the sunset. That night, enormous lightning bolts tore through the dark heavens, while the booming continued. Later we were to learn that some of the infrasonic shocks travelled as far as Colorado in the United States, where they were recorded as comparable in magnitude to the largest nuclear explosions.

I remember standing on the beach with a group of neighbours, in awed silence. It was not fear that we experienced, as we somehow never felt threatened by 'our' volcanoes, which had indeed erupted many times before, but utter amazement at the spectacle unfolding before our eyes. The powerful explosions, which could be felt as much as heard, etched themselves in my memory forever that night. To this day I stop in my tracks, still hoping I will hear another exploding volcano, whenever any distant thud can be heard.

A few days later my father and I sailed on the *Kim* to a deep bay indenting the midriff of Isabela Island, Cartago Bay, from where we could get a clear, unimpeded view of Fernandina. Dark and symmetrical in the distance, the island looked as stately and unmoved as it had six months before when we'd anchored at its very base. Fernandina was not giving away its secret so easily.

And then the scientists came. Within less than a month a team of vulcanologists had mobilized to scrutinize the event under the leadership of Dr Tom Simkin, whose name and friendship over the decades that followed were to become inseparable in my mind from that of Fernandina. The team caused quite a stir by interrogating all the resident eyewitnesses before heading out to climb the still-rumbling volcano, sharing their findings when they returned. What transpired was that the entire caldera, formerly about six kilometres across and 600 metres deep, had collapsed inward into what they estimated to be a magma void of some two cubic kilometres.

Overleaf: A scene of utter tranquillity permeates the caldera lake in 1975, as white-cheeked pintails feed on aquatic insects.

Massive, thundering rock falls spontaneously detach from the unstable caldera walls.

After every new eruption the wildlife must strive to readjust to its ever-changing environment.

While this process is how all calderas are formed, it is such a rare event that this was only the second caldera collapse recorded in human history.

Perhaps the most bitter disappointment of my teenage years came when my father prudently and adamantly decided that it was not a good idea for me to climb Fernandina with the team of vulcanologists, whom I'd begged to take me along. Their stories upon returning fired in me a lifelong fascination for the wildest of wild places, where the earth remains untamed. Two and a half more years were to pass before I was able to set eyes on Fernandina's incredible caldera, and in the decade that followed no two years would pass without my returning again and again. I climbed the volcano from some of the more forbidding, virtually untrodden, approaches and criss-crossed the island twice. In all, I have visited the caldera a dozen times and descended into it on half those occasions, possibly more than any other person. In my mind the volcano has acquired almost mythical proportions. Like a living being it evolves and changes, its mood swings ranging from the serene to sombre, nerve-tingling violence. For me, to visit Fernandina is to take a step back in time, to a place where the land is still being formed and unique species still bask in raw ecological balance;

to venture into its awesome caldera is to witness the birthplace of the earth, where wildlife constantly strives to readjust to, and take best advantage of, the dramatically evolving landscape.

In 1975 I arranged transport on a small fishing boat and spent a magical month with my parents and brother on Fernandina. After camping for two weeks among the sea lions, fur seals, penguins, flightless cormorants and marine iguanas of Cape Douglas, we spent an additional two weeks exploring the island's highest and youngest reaches. Little had changed since the 1968 caldera collapse. The entire south-western half of the volcano's rim and upper slopes had been transformed into a grey and ochre moonscape where volcanic ash had blanketed the land, smoothing and rounding all contours and obliterating all life at the time. Orange-coloured land iguanas, heftier than their marine cousins, now wandered resolutely across this desolate landscape, while pretty Galapagos doves flocked to the dripping moisture exuded by a string of steaming fumaroles.

Thousands of land iguanas live on Fernandina. Here a group of females share a male's lava burrow in the mating season.

Having rarely, if ever, seen people Galapagos hawks are insatiably curious.

Land iguanas on the rim of the volcano rely on juicy cactus pads for water.

We explored much of the caldera rim, and several giant caldera benches, monstrously fissured and pitted, giving the impression they could soon slide down into the yawning gape of the caldera itself. Indeed, massive rock avalanches would develop at any time of day or night, thundering down in clouds of dust and crashing stone. The caldera was far from settled since the 1968 collapse, avalanche scars painting long grey streaks nearly 1,000 metres from rim to floor as house-sized boulders plunged into the blue mineral lake below. These moments of charged power contrasted eerily with the otherwise complete tranquillity that prevailed. Every daybreak commenced in utter calm. Not the slightest breeze stirred the clear, cool air as the sun rose bright and warm over the caldera's brim, its deep red rays creeping tentatively down the sheer walls into the lingering twilight below, the lake's windless surface mirroring purple dawn shadows. At nearly 1,500 metres elevation, with the moist cloud layers settled considerably lower along the island's outer slope, the air felt totally different from the coast, crisp and dry with night-time temperatures sometimes dropping to

Two months after the 1978 eruption, the cycle of life, and the pintails, return to the caldera lake.

near-freezing. From the scant vegetation to the north, land iguanas emerged from their deep burrows dug in the firm volcanic ash to bask in the sun's warmth, while finches and mockingbirds busied themselves feeding on dry grass heads or diminutive endemic tomatoes. Curious Galapagos hawks, having rarely, if ever, seen humans, followed us about for hours.

Each day that we spent on the rim the mysterious caldera beckoned. Eventually we could resist no longer and decided to push our explorations further. The descent was not easy as the volcanic layers of ash, rubble and lava were almost vertical and extremely friable, and should an accident occur there would be absolutely no chance of rescue. After a day of shimmying and scrambling, using meagre shrubbery as handholds and lowering our heavy pack on a piece of twine, we finally followed a steep ravine, cut deep into the thick ash layers, down to the lake shore. The setting here was truly surreal. The contrast between the raw grandeur of the surroundings and the vibrancy of a teeming wildlife community was nothing short of unbelievable. On the land not a blade of grass grew, yet the lake, so heavily laden in mineral salts it was unfit for human consumption, produced a thick algal soup which in turn nurtured millions of aquatic insects. Varieties of insects, ranging from tiny gnats to swarms of dragon-

A 1988 rim eruption showered several metres of scorching hot scoria over prime land iguana habitat, burying them alive.

flies, supported flocks of black-necked stilts and hundreds of white-cheeked pintails, by far the largest population in Galapagos. The lake shores were matted in spider webs entrapping hatching insects, while predacious little lava lizards were themselves preyed upon by Galapagos snakes. Surrounded on all sides by towering walls from which stones routinely crumbled and crashed, this thriving assemblage of life was completely dependent on the rich productivity of the volcanic lake, all the more astounding as only two years before all life in the caldera had been annihilated by an intense bout of activity.

On no fewer than four separate occasions during the '70s, lava flows issued from various fissure systems encircling the caldera and poured down into the lake, each time causing its waters to boil and extinguishing all life. In 1977, on one of my many fact-finding missions for Tom Simkin, I found myself once again inside the caldera, within seven days of a new lava flow which had spread long smouldering black fingers into the lake. In a fit of reckless enthusiasm, my companions and I paddled a tiny inflatable boat

A massive landslide and lava flow partially filled in the lake in 1988, causing spectacular steam explosions.

Talons to the fore, a pale coloured juvenile hawk swoops on its prey.

across the now steaming lake's surface to the new lava delta, the water temperature around us climbing to 78°C. To our amazement we found flocks of pintails sitting listlessly along the dark and lifeless shores, quietly starving to death rather than departing for another island. Yet at that time Fernandina still guarded what I like to think of as its most amazing biological secret.

I returned to the caldera several more times in the following years. On various occasions I had noticed surprising amounts of land iguana traffic along the very edge of the caldera, particularly on an early visit in July 1974. Indeed, a German herpetologist named Dagmar Werner had discovered that female land iguanas living in patches of vegetation on the outer slopes of the volcano migrated to the rim to nest in warm ash surrounding fumarole activity. But nothing prepared me for what awaited my next caldera descent in October 1982. Dozens of Galapagos hawks, descended from the rim for the occasion, were swooping down in the dry ravines, feeding on tiny land iguana hatchlings that were emerging from

Awaiting the morning sun, a Galapagos hawk has descended to
the caldera floor in pursuit of iguana hatchlings.

nests in the barren ash beds. Their chances of survival seemed almost as remote as if they had hatched on the moon, being several kilometres and nearly 1,000 vertical metres from the nearest food supply and plant cover. Dashing from the meagre shelter of one boulder to the next, they responded to an inexorable drive to reach high ground, somehow aware that they must escape the caldera as soon as possible. Although extremely wary and well camouflaged, 20 centimetres of baby reptile hardly seemed an adequate match for the volcanic setting and ravenous raptors.

Two years later I was able to witness the extraordinary migration that the female land iguanas undertake to deposit their eggs, not only on the rim, as Dagmar had observed, but down in the very maw of the volcano. The scene was astounding. A new eruption had added more lava which was still quite hot, yet wherever any of the underlying volcanic ash was exposed female iguanas were digging, fighting and searching for nest sites. The level of activity was frenetic, in spite of the intense heat caused both by the recent lava and the inherent sun-trap effect of the deep, bowl-shaped caldera. With many of the nests only one or two metres apart, dirt flung by one excavating female would land in another's burrow. Open-mouthed, head-bobbing threat displays were frequent, with occasional aggressive chases. I watched one female pursue a rival with such vigour, riding on its back and biting its neck, that when she finally stopped some 30 metres distant she was too disoriented to retrace her steps and relocate her own nest, where several freshly laid eggs remained exposed. She spent the rest of the day unsuccessfully checking every burrow entrance, incurring the wrath of the occupants.

To reach this location the female iguanas had travelled for days up the flanks of the volcano, across barren lava flows and ash fields, along the caldera rim and down the precipitous caldera wall, dodging rockfalls and traversing crevasses and boulder slopes in scorching heat. Within a few days of laying their eggs they would begin to retrace their steps, a trip which might take them a couple of weeks. In three months' time their young would have to follow suit. I could not begin to fathom what selective pressures could ever have moulded such improbable behaviour, especially when the dangers of rockfalls and hawk predation were considered, or an entire nesting season's product being wiped clean by the unfortunate timing

Shrinking fast, the last of the caldera lake sublimates into swirls of steam after the 1988 eruption.

of a new eruption. Precisely such a fate befell the iguanas in the 1988 nesting season. News of another eruption had brought me back to the top of the volcano in September of that year, a time when the eggs on the caldera floor would have been nearly ready to hatch. However, when I peered over the edge, I could not believe my eyes: the caldera was disfigured beyond recognition. A huge portion of the eastern rim of the volcano, where a large tract of vegetation now lay blanketed in a thick layer of fresh black scoria, had broken loose and slumped down into the caldera. This massive landslide had sloshed the entire lake out of its bed and part way up the opposite wall. What water was left was in the process of boiling away fast, with yet another new lava flow covering most of the floor.

A few months later the lake had completely vanished, leaving only two mud-filled puddles barely a few metres across. Where pintails had once paddled and iguanas had fought for prime nesting sites, I now walked in a landscape befitting the great deserts of Mars. Huge piles of volcanic rubble lay scattered in heaps and ridges as in an open mine, and pit craters pock-marked the ground. Thick layers of lakebed sediment, liberally redistributed by the turmoil of the last activity and plastered on all contours of the jumbled terrain, had dried out in eerie, concentric, cracked patterns encircling every hill or hollow. Twenty years after the massive event of 1968 Fernandina had reached another turning point. The beautiful lake was gone, perhaps forever.

By 1989 the caldera floor is a moonscape of dried sediment, the beautiful lake reduced to remnant puddles.

Caldera Migration

On what seems like a suicidal mission, each July female land iguanas converge from around the volcano to nest inside its warm caldera. Some may walk ten days to reach the rim (below), then begin to search for a route down its vertiginous and constantly collapsing walls (near right). Running the risk of landslides and untimely eruptions, they finally reach prime nesting grounds in the thick layers of sun-baked volcanic ash on the caldera floor (centre right) were they dig the nesting burrows (far right) in a flurry of activity that lasts a few short days. They spend hours covering up all evidence of the nest (right, below) and several more days guarding the spot against latecomers before setting off on the home journey, a round trip which may take a month or more. The caldera seems a formidable place to start life as a baby iguana, especially when numerous nests are destroyed by volcanic activity, and hatchlings crossing bare ground fall prey to hawks.

A giant tortoise may wander far around the volcano's rim, here filled with morning clouds.

8 WHERE GIANTS ROAM
The Tortoises of Alcedo Volcano

Dawn breaks slowly and life is peaceful on Alcedo Volcano. The central and lowest of the chain of shield volcanoes that make up Isabela Island, this is a very different place from Fernandina, only 50 kilometres to the west. Far from the harsh beauty and vibrant energy of Fernandina's volcanic power, Alcedo is infinitely gentler, softened by age and mellowed through long periods of slumber. Still very much a young and active volcano, Alcedo is nonetheless in that stage of life approaching what is in vulcanology termed 'morphological decline'. Its contour is substantially flatter than Fernandina's, its rim a low and narrow crest, and its caldera wide and shallow. And while a thick blanket of old pumice speaks of violent explosive activity in the past, today it is generously cloaked in vegetation. Recent activity has been limited to a small flow far down on its outer flank, plus extensive steam and sulphur fumaroles dotting its slumping caldera benches.

As night gives way, the first signs of day — streaks of gold and crimson — spill over the far rim of the sleeping caldera, six kilometres across from where I sit. Below, a soft blanket of fog lies as yet unstirred by the morning breeze. Hesitantly, the slow song of a Darwin's finch breaks the silence, while a Galapagos hawk, up early, soars in tight circles over the steady plume of a steaming fumarole. Another day begins in a place that speaks of time immemorial.

Pushing and shoving marks a predilection for spending the night in mud wallows.

Close to my tent is a cluster of several dozen giant tortoises resting, stock still, in a shallow rain pond, like so many wave-polished boulders in a tide pool. As the brightening sky burnishes their dew-laden backs with fiery hues, one or two begin to stir, rippling the mirror surface of the water. A slow hiss, the creaking of two carapaces rubbing together like the sound of an old leather saddle, bubbles rising from primitive vegetarian guts — so begins the day of the giant tortoise.

A massive male sits closest to me, immersed in his tick-cleansing mud wallow to the edge of his shell, eyes and nostrils barely above waterline. His head rises like a sentry at the thud of human footsteps, his wrinkled throat pumping slowly in and out as he tests the air for the new scent. Moist eyes glistening, his dark gaze falls upon the human intruder, steady as the centuries he may have seen pass. No-one knows just how long a Galapagos giant tortoise may live in the wild, since no person has been in these islands long enough to see one live to its natural old age. Possibly this one was already here when young Charles Darwin himself visited the

Clouds still fill the caldera as a tortoise heads onto the grassy rim to feed at sunrise.

The rainy season is a time of renewal: a giant tortoise starts the day in a green pool.

A sudden downpour freshens the giant tortoise's ancient world.

During the rains a tortoise drinks copiously to survive the dry months ahead.

Under the day's gathering rain clouds, a large male leaves the night pools to feed.

islands more than 160 years ago. No matter, this old tortoise has watched the equatorial seasons slowly go by, has seen volcanic eruptions and the rains come and go so many times that the passing of years hardly seems relevant. He yawns, a wide, unhurried tortoise yawn. It is the rainy season now and the volcano is resplendent once again in lush greenery, and it is time for his morning feed. Deliberately he rises, lifting his elephantine feet from the thick mud with suctioning sounds, 200 kilograms of lumbering reptile clambering slowly out of his night hollow. He rocks slightly as he walks, his large toe-nails, needle sharp when young but now round and worn smooth, pug the ground. A short distance away he settles down to graze the tender meadows that have sprung from the volcanic pumice in response to the recent rains.

With the warm morning sun burning away the last wisps of fog, every tortoise in the caldera is busily grazing, while already making their way toward stands of shade-giving trees and shrubs to escape the escalating heat of the day. By noon, even Darwin's finch songs have all but ceased and each shady bush harbours several dozing tortoises, heads and legs lying limp on the ground. As the sun tips toward the west, and the air cools slightly at the approach of an impending cloudburst, one by one they emerge from their siestas, yawning and stretching their legs, maybe stopping by a pool for a long, slow draught of muddy water. Finally, another two or three hours of grazing reverses their morning wanderings, ending the day with a free-for-all of pushing and shoving back into the heavily churned, sun-warmed, mud wallows.

Alcedo Volcano is home to the largest population of Galapagos giant tortoises remaining today, numbering between 4,000 and 5,000. I made my first visit here in 1969, when I was only 15, a short, magical incursion into a timeless, circular caldera world where giant reptiles still roam as in aeons past. These tortoises were the subject of my first published pictures, and so my passion for photography was fired. Over 25 years I have returned dozens of times, often staying for a week or two, living off what I could carry on my back, including water which, if you don't bring what you need, can only be obtained with luck from infrequent rains. Over the years I feel I have lived both the tortoise day and the tortoise season.

Reptiles are reputedly unintelligent organisms that respond to the mere basic stimuli needed for survival. Yet from a naturalist's perspective the

Selecting favourite herbs, an old tortoise grazes the caldera floor.

The morning sun is slow to burn through the fog-filled caldera.

behaviour, memory and inherent curiosity of the giant tortoise are all utterly intriguing. They travel known paths to seasonal haunts, certain individuals favouring particular locations year after year. While many lead sedate lives, others demonstrate real wanderlust, sometimes travelling ten or 20 kilometres beyond their normal habitat. They remember the exact location of likely water-holes, hurrying to the site when the first raindrops of the season hit, pressing their noses in dusty hollows in anticipation of the water they know will soon gather. If a sleeping tortoise senses an unusual vibration in the ground, as in the footfall of an approaching person, it will raise its head and scan the surroundings, sniffing the air audibly even though reptiles, in theory, have poor olfactory senses. If they encounter an unknown object they nudge it, sniff it, then test it by biting, even if this object happens to be an unmoving person's foot. This inquisitiveness is so persistent, with inevitably destructive results, that I found the only way to protect my camp from shredding and trampling was to build a low log fence around it.

The rainy season is the period of greatest activity on Alcedo, a time when a verdant sheen tints the land, and food and drink abound for the

The sound of mating echoes around the caldera.

At the end of the day, tortoises drift across the caldera floor, grazing as they go.

primeval grazers. Large numbers of tortoises congregate from as far afield as the outer slopes of the volcano and travel down from the steep rim onto the caldera floor, where temporary rain ponds form and open meadows are maintained, in part, by their heavy grazing. Although capable of surviving many months without food or water, at this time tortoises graze relentlessly, and drink large amounts several times a day. I once had a half-grown tortoise visit my camp as I was collecting water from the first rain shower of the season. Every time the two litre pot I had placed under the corner of a tarpaulin filled, he returned to drain it, eventually downing nearly ten litres in under an hour — and this was only a medium-sized tortoise.

The rainy season is also the peak of mating for the ancient tortoises. Everywhere in the caldera the eerie, rhythmic groans of mounted males ring out throughout the days, the only true sound the tortoises ever emit. As if perpetuating time itself, mating may take up to an hour to complete. The coy females almost invariably give the males a good run, sometimes plunging into undergrowth where the much larger males become snagged on low branches. Occasionally a male will stop a female by threatening to

Surrounded by fumaroles, mating takes place in a small rim pool.

123

bite her and towering in front of her, or even by nipping at her legs. It is not unusual for a reluctant, pinned-down female to spin around on the spot in a last ditch effort to foil mating.

Ritualized, aggressive displays break out frequently during the breeding season, consisting of gaping at each other while raising heads as high as possible. Behavioural studies have shown that males are not territorial, nor are they dominant over each other or over females, yet aggressive displays occur at random and during any activity. Sometimes aggression is shown by one animal while the other turns away, or it may be returned in kind. This can take place between males or between females, or even from a female to a male. Invariably the one that towers highest over the other wins the argument, although uneven terrain may contribute more to the outcome than size alone. Sometimes the defeated individual, who withdraws his head and turns away, is rammed or his legs bitten by the victor. Yet the same two tortoises may resume grazing side by side only minutes later.

As in the rest of Galapagos, the rains on Alcedo are entirely unpredictable, sometimes starting in January and lasting four months, other years consisting of just one or two showers in March or April, and occasionally failing altogether. As the ground dries and the vegetation shrivels, the tortoises' predilection for mud wallowing remains undiminished. Competition increases daily for space in the fast-shrinking ponds. Churning, shoving and ramming marks the end of each day, as puddles laden with dung and green algal slime turn into an ever thicker slurry. Still the tortoises drink the last of the congealing mud as if aware that there will be no more for months.

As the year advances and drought and cool *garua* mists shroud the volcano, many tortoises head for the caldera rim, where fog may condense on moss-laden trees and collect, drip by drip, in small puddles. They frequent time-polished rock slabs which they know collect small amounts of nightly drizzle. And mostly they wait, digging wallows of deep dust when there is no mud, possibly in an effort to deter tick infestations. Darwin's finches, feeling a dearth of insects in this season, may approach a tortoise with exaggerated hops, a signal to which the reptile responds by stretching neck and legs to full height allowing the birds access to the blood-filled parasites.

During long droughts tortoises search for damp earth
from steaming fumaroles to alleviate their thirst.

A ritualized aggressive display consists of an
intimidating gape while stretching as high as possible.

The height of the dry season is also when the gravid females migrate to specific nesting sites in the warmer parts of the caldera to lay their eggs. They travel down well-worn pathways for many miles, digging their nests in pockets of dry earth and covering them with crusts of clay mixed with urine and dung. All being well, four to six months of solar incubation later the young emerge unaided, only weeks before the beginning of a new rainy season.

Like a relic from times when reptiles ruled the world unchallenged, the seasons of the giant tortoise have trickled by unhurriedly on Alcedo Volcano for hundreds of thousands of years. No doubt volcanic eruptions changed the face of the island, and Galapagos hawks preyed on a few hatchlings, but the pressures for change have made little impression on an animal that may take a decade or two to reach breeding age, and a century or more to run the course of its life. For me, a week spent on Alcedo Volcano is a visit to a dreamland where giants roam.

Still, evolutionary pressures did leave their mark, albeit subtle, on the giant tortoises. Before man arrived, 14 distinct populations existed in isolation on different islands or volcanoes. Although all belonged to just one species, each one had developed individual characteristics to suit the conditions it lived in. The most extreme adaptations are found on the smallest, driest islands where the reptilian grazers turned to browsers instead of grazers. Looking quite different from the 'dome' type tortoises of Alcedo, these 'saddlebacks' evolved to reach high in the arid scrub, plucking leafy branches or juicy cactus pads for moisture.

Nowhere has the balance between the giant tortoise and its insular environment remained as untouched for as long as on Alcedo. First the inroads from meat-hungry sailors decimated the most accessible populations. Then a whole bevy of introduced mammals (either released intentionally, such as goats to provide easy game, or accidentally, as with rats and cats) began to compete for food or prey on the young. Each volcano on Isabela has a distinct race of tortoise, as well as its own set of problems from introduced feral mammals, separated as they are by extensive, low-lying lava fields. On some islands pigs and dogs killed tortoises up to several years old, on another rats annihilated all eggs and hatchlings. Goats and cattle converted lush forests to bare fields, where crucial shade-giving trees have been reduced to stumps. Under these pressures some tortoises became

A peaceful afternoon siesta in a warm pool amid rim fumaroles.

extinct last century, and the Pinta Island race was reduced to a single male as late as the 1970s, now dubbed 'Lonesome George' and held in captivity in the dwindling hopes of finding him a mate. In recent years captive breeding and releasing young tortoises large enough to avoid predation, together with intensive campaigns to eliminate feral animals, have reversed the decline of several tortoise types. Both these programmes, the hallmark of conservation work in Galapagos, have been steadfastly carried out for nearly four decades by the Galapagos National Park Service and Charles Darwin Research Station. Ironically perhaps, the future of the giant tortoise will be far more challenging to manage than in the recent past, with human pressures and conflicting interests growing rapidly. Even the tortoises of Alcedo are no longer safe, with the sudden arrival of expanding goat populations invading their caldera haven from the south.

In the sad tale of tortoise decline, there is one mystery which has fired the imagination like none other, yet is unlikely ever to be resolved, casting us back momentarily to mythical Fernandina Island. On 6 April 1906, high on the slope of the volcano, an intrepid herpetologist named Rollo Beck discovered the largest saddleback tortoise ever known, which he dutifully killed, gutted and collected as a specimen for his museum. Its remains were later named *Geochelone elephantopus phantastica*, the 'Fantastic, elephant-footed, ancient tortoise'. What the indomitable Rollo did not know is that no-one would ever again see another live 'Fantastic tortoise'. We are left to presume that a particularly devastating volcanic eruption had already obliterated the remaining 'Fantastic tortoise' population, perhaps covering vital nesting grounds with unyielding lava flows that made recovery impossible. Must we conclude, then, that through the excruciatingly slow ticking of geologic time, of volcanic developments and evolutionary adaptations, Mr. Beck stumbled his way up Fernandina at the precise moment, that infinitely small blip in the history of life on earth, when one race of animals was on the eve of a totally natural extinction?

Saddleback tortoises have evolved on arid islands where they have become browsers rather than grazers, Pinzon.

Feathered Neighbours

Alcedo Volcano is home to a number of endemic birds who associate in various ways with the giant tortoises. Juvenile hawks still roaming without territories sometimes gather here from afar in amazing numbers, soaring on the thermal updraughts above the caldera (below), or perching in the rim vegetation (top, near right). Inside the caldera they sometimes choose the boulder-like back of a tortoise as a convenient vantage from which to hunt large rainy season crickets, even if the tortoise is moving (top, centre right). Very young tortoises may make a hawk meal, but by the time they are two or three years old they only elicit curiosity (top, far right). Darwin's finches, particularly the small ground finch here eating cactus pollen (bottom, centre), are also abundant. During the dry season when tortoise ticks are rife but finch food scarce, they clean the posturing reptiles of their parasites in a mutually beneficial relationship (bottom, far right).

Surrounded by creole fish, leather bass and yellowtail surgeonfish, a male green turtle approaches a cleaning station, Wolf.

9 WHALES, SHARKS AND VAMPIRE FINCHES

Encounters Beyond the Outpost Isles

As the decades trickled by, Galapagos were swept up into the ever-accelerating, man-made time warp that governs today's world. In 1976 I met and married a young National Park planner from New England. Alan was an ardent conservationist who dedicated his life to preserving the world's wild places. In Galapagos he worked tirelessly to help the National Park Service in its uphill battle to protect and restore the islands, first as a United Nations consultant, then as a Peace Corps volunteer, and eventually on his own time. He taught me to look at the world as a delicate bubble of interwoven life strands, one that man is increasingly in danger of bursting irretrievably. Together we worked with teams of National Park wardens to exterminate feral goats and dogs, and to design nature trails that would minimize the impact of the budding tourist industry. We also travelled to many parts of North, Central and South America. But through the seven years of our marriage we also grew apart. I was increasingly drawn to spending time in the wildest places I could find, to query the infinite details of the natural world, whereas Alan's vocation lay in working with people on the topics that consumed him. Even when we spent time hiking and camping, which we did often, we seemed to be looking at the world through totally separate portholes. Eventually, though still the best of friends, we agreed to go our separate ways.

Deep offshore waters, where sea lions join whales and sharks, are full of surprises.

Never seen near shore, an olive ridley turtle is a pelagic visitor from tropical northern waters.

A green turtle drifts along a deep, current-scoured sea wall amid schooling Cortez chubs, Wolf.

The year 1983 was a tumultuous one in many respects. It was the year the 'Super El Niño', or the 'El Niño of the Century' as it was often called, struck with a vengeance that took the western world completely by surprise, with monstrous storms and floods devastating the coast of the Americas from California to Chile. In Galapagos deluges of rain fell daily for nine interminable months, turning the islands from their normal semi-desert condition to a roaring tropical jungle. Giant cacti toppled and disappeared under tangles of runaway vines, torrents and waterfalls cascaded from the cliffs of Santa Fe and over the lava fields of Fernandina. Beaches were swept inland and flamingo lagoons destroyed as sea-levels rose to unprecedented heights. Sea lions, fur seals and Galapagos penguins died of disease and starvation, while most seabirds headed out to the high seas in search of food. Marine iguanas were hit hardest, first by the vicious pounding of incessant swells, making feeding grounds inaccessible, then by the replacement of normal algae species with indigestible kinds, mortality rates ranging between 45 and 70 per cent in some colonies.

This was also the year that I met Mark. A diver and biology student from the north of England, on contract as a naturalist for one of the local tour companies, he had fallen in love with island life during his two year stint. During the height of El Niño, chance would have us co-lead the first-ever group of visitors to hike into the interior of several of Isabela's wild volcanoes. Non-stop rain, waist-deep flooded trails, walls of impenetrable vegetation and grumbling, exhausted clients tested our enthusiasm and stamina. Yet in spite, or perhaps because of, these less than ideal conditions, two weeks together were enough to discover in each other our *alter egos*. During that exhausting trip we found time to share our zest for life, swimming in the pristine caldera lake of Cerro Azul, exploring huge solfataras (sulphur-encrusted fumaroles) and riding like the wind among the wild horses of Sierra Negra, and befriending a day-old wild donkey on Alcedo.

In the years that followed, together we broadened our explorations and discovered a new passion for photography. From time to time we ventured away from Galapagos, travelling to the seabird-rich Falkland Islands, the frozen shores of Antarctica and the flower-decked tundra of the Arctic, to the mountains of Tibet and New Zealand, and the rainforests of Indonesia and Peru. Meanwhile, the decade had left its mark on my

Schooling hammerhead sharks appear mysteriously with small groups of courting black jacks, Darwin.

Hammerheads are extremely shy and poorly understood, visitors from unknown wanderings, Wolf.

family in Galapagos. My father, who had never known a day of illness in his life, whose mind had been dedicated to resolving mysteries and exploring the unknown, began to falter and shy away from the unfamiliar. He no longer felt confident to sail the *Inti*, even though he had designed and built her himself. Eventually he made a self-diagnosis of Alzheimer's disease, which tragically proved correct. After a few, mercifully short years of decline, he died at home in 1991. He was just 66 years old.

My Mom rebuilt her life alone, never losing the indomitable family spirit. Two years later my brother and his second wife, Martha, a pretty Ecuadorian girl with Chinese ancestry on her grandmother's side, brought the first and only grandchild into the family. With golden skin, straw-coloured hair and almond eyes, Natalie came into the world a smiling blend of her diverse backgrounds, and in her young years has espoused her Galapagos environment as joyfully as my brother and I had done over 30 years earlier.

Through the years of my father's illness the *Inti* had lain idle at anchor, though her 20-year-old tropical oak hull was still as good as new. My brother, who once chartered her out to visitors with his first wife, had now settled ashore with his family, yet my mother rejected all notion of putting her up for sale. It was thanks to her steadfast views that Mark and I were able to take our Galapagos adventures to new extremes. We refurbished the *Inti* and headed for the outer fringes of the islands.

Our favourite place in recent years became the remote outpost isles of Wolf and Darwin, some 140 kilometres north of the rest of the archipelago. On many trips by ourselves, we took turns diving alone along sheer, current-scoured walls where great schools of hammerhead sharks cruised by, watching us shyly. Drifting in from the blue void, green turtles gathered around cleaning stations where angel fish would rid them of skin parasites, and on rare occasions a huge whale shark would glide slowly past. Massive feeding frenzies would develop offshore, boobies, dolphins, sea lions, tuna and unbelievable numbers of silky sharks mingling in pursuit of tight schools of small fish.

Above the water-line these towering, though small, islands rose as

Overleaf: *Semi-pelagic steel pompanos are joined along a surf-beaten wall by a reef-dwelling king angelfish, Wolf.*

133

The ocean is charged with life during an offshore feeding frenzy, as silky sharks close in on a tightly balled cluster of juvenile creole fish, Wolf.

precipitously as they plunged down into the depths, their countless layers of prehistoric lava undercut by wave action. The sound of tens of thousands of seabirds filled the air as they occupied every ledge and bush. Boobies, frigates, tropic birds, swallow-tailed gulls, all milled about constantly. We managed to visit the only nesting colony of sooty terns found in Galapagos, restricted to the near-inaccessible plateau on the top of Darwin. Perhaps the most amazing of all, however, were the little sharp-billed ground finches, a species of Darwin's finch also found on other islands but having developed a most unusual habit on these isolated islands. Here, and only here, they obtain their protein when food is scarce in times of drought, by pecking at the base of nesting boobies' wing and tail feathers, carefully drawing blood without leaving much of an injury. This startling behaviour has earned them the name 'vampire finches'.

For two seasons Mark and I had worked as naturalists on a whale-watching ship in the Mexican waters of Baja California, an experience which opened our eyes to the realm of the open ocean. No longer was it just a

In deep offshore waters, sharks, dolphins, rainbow runners, tuna and other predators converge on their prey from above and below, Wolf.

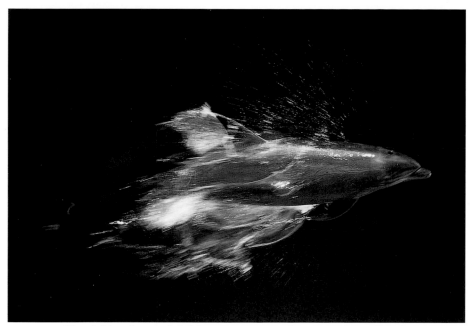

Playful bottlenose dolphins are common in waters just offshore, and in between islands.

stretch to be crossed in order to reach a far shore, as it had been during my childhood years, it now became a destination in itself.

Here we spotted unusual petrels straying up from faraway Antarctic waters, and encountered feeding whales and huge schools of leaping dolphins. Whenever we had a chance, one of us would leap over the side to spend a few magical moments sharing the trackless realm of these mysterious denizens of the deep blue. One day I was able to swim with two orcas, snorkelling down to watch as they preyed on a hapless stingray. Near the lone monolith of Roca Redonda I shared the joys of bow-riding with a group of playful bottlenose dolphins, hanging on to the bobstay below the bowsprit, as Mark revved up the engine until the dolphins rode the wave just in front of my mask.

Contacts with visiting whale researchers had taught us how to track whale and dolphin sounds underwater, making it possible to follow their movements as they travel through the ocean. Days and nights melded together as Mark and I breathed the utter simplicity of life between sea and

A passing visitor, a male orca carefully pulls a stingray by the tip of the tail out from under a boulder, Santa Cruz.

sky, our attention focused on the unseen lives of pods of whales plying the deep. With the aid of a home-made acoustic reflector holding a tiny hydrophone (an underwater microphone) we followed them round the clock as they fed and cruised slowly below. Time seemed to linger indefinitely, the world was shut out, and even today by just closing my eyes I can revisit those corners of my mind as if I was still there.

It was the second watch of the night, the brief equatorial twilight long since gone. Our little sloop lay wallowing some 90 kilometres south-west of Fernandina Island, wrapped in stillness, cradled between smooth Pacific swells rising and falling gently like a sleeping giant. A billion stars hovered above, their perfect reflection upon the water blending heavens and ocean into one. Our sails, quite helpless, shifted with a slap. Otherwise there was only silence. The sea might be as empty of life as the interplanetary void. Yet below us they glided, the mighty sperm whales that have fascinated mankind since time immemorial, because of their size, their oil, their teeth or their wisdom. Through our directional hydrophone, we could now eavesdrop on their busy world, gauge the direction and speed of their travel, and try to imagine their occupation as their sounds rang through the night. Clickety-click — click — click — click — click — . About a dozen whales, all speaking in rhythmic, codified, sonar voices, some slow and stately, others so quick, almost creaking. Hunting? Playing? Conversing? Probably we would never know. Even with the earphones clamped tightly to my head this very thought lifted my spirit. We were not, after all, so distantly superior, in control and able to satisfy our curiosity at will. Thankfully, mankind still has limitations. Paradoxically, I felt closer to the unreachable whales at that moment.

Phwoooosh. Vast, powerful lungs emptied into the night air, half a kilometre to port. Like an echo, another blow rose to starboard, then another, faint but clearly audible in the stillness, over one kilometre ahead. Others joined them. The entire pod was surfacing, blowing again and again, replenishing the oxygen in their muscle and blood in preparation for another 50 minute foray into the depths.

The nearest whale was less than 100 metres away, on our starboard quarter. Each breath drew nearer, a two-tone bellow: huge, unhurried exhalations followed instantly by the cavernous echo of air rushing to refill

Bottlenose dolphins love to bowride, jostling for the best position even with a person riding with them, Roca Redonda.

A sperm whale raises its fluke gracefully, descending into the abyss on a dive that may last almost an hour.

the spacious chest. Phwooo-hhooosh. Venus was setting, casting her shimmering reflection upon the water. Etched in black against this luminescent puddle a blunt head appeared. Gliding along the surface not ten metres astern, the whale moved slowly alongside, about the same length as our ten metre hull. Huge flukes rose in a gentle arch under the starlight. Droplets tinkled like broken crystal. Slowly the dark shape slid beneath the water. The surface settled, the whale was gone. Gone in pursuit of phosphorescent squid in the abyss?

For ten days and nights we followed the sperm whales on that trip near the edge of the Galapagos Platform. We traced their movements through dense fog, with swallow-tailed gulls, like white ghosts in the night, hovering about our mast-head light. We photographed their personalized fluke patterns in the blazing, noonday sun and we watched storm petrels feed on the thin strands of their shedded skin. We travelled 1,600 kilometres in search of the whales. Yet never could we come closer to a true understanding than I did on that starlit night, alone at the helm.

Another time, another trip: all day the whales had been travelling south-east into the stiff tradewinds, spouting sporadically across the horizon.

Then, suddenly, a dark, bulbous head appeared alongside, followed in the next few minutes by 14 more, rolling, spy-hopping, playing at the surface it seemed. In an instant I had grabbed my camera, mask and snorkel and was swimming toward the ebony backs glistening between the waves. My head felt tossed about while the steep chop insisted on breaking over my snorkel. The nearest island I knew lay many kilometres beyond the horizon. I did not dwell on the thought that perhaps I was not welcome here.

Soon I became aware of a presence to my right. Looming out of the blue-green mist several great foreheads were approaching, like the steep prows of ships. To be afraid seemed an absurd consideration. At that moment I felt as though I had stopped existing as a human being anyway. I was a mere spirit floating somewhere in the twilight between heaven and earth, greeted by another spirit, a blessing from the ocean. Slowly the whales swerved. They glided by, no more than five metres in front of me, a calf and several females, rolling slightly to get a better look. I could see their white belly markings and jaw outlines, their dimpled abdomens and, above all, their querying left eyes. I reminded myself to take pictures. Two more strokes of the great flukes and they disappeared into the distant depths. Suddenly I felt very human and very alone. Below me, shafts of sun tentatively probed a thousand fathoms of water. My eyes could focus on nothing but the fleeting dance of light in the now empty sea. I looked up and slowly began swimming back toward our boat, looking frail between the waves.

The last time I visited the sperm whale's world was during a dive off the north-western tip of Fernandina, at the very edge of the Galapagos Platform, where it drops almost vertically to more than 3,000 metres. The food chain here is intense, from dense phytoplankton bloom all the way to deep water squid on which the sperm whales feed. Mark and I dropped in less than 300 metres from shore. The water was distinctly chilly and so laden with life that we could not see each other more than a metre apart. Through the soup we descended, vaguely aware of turtles gliding around us. Normally very cautious in our scuba-diving ventures, this time we agreed through signs to press our exploration further than we'd ever done before, to see what lay beyond the murk. At a depth of 25 metres we reached bottom, a steep lava slope plunging forever deeper, where harlequin hogfish

Where upwellings are strongest, endemic black coral, reef fish
and other invertebrates abound, Bainbridge.

A pod of female sperm whales appears briefly from the fathomless depths.

played. At 35 metres the colour of the water had changed from deep green to dark brown, at 45 to almost total blackness. Then at 50 metres the world was transformed. The temperature dropped to around 10°C and the visibility opened up to a limitless blue-black clarity, the quality of glacial ice. The entire slope shimmered dimly in a lacework of black coral inhabited by deep water butterflyfish.

We had entered the heart of the Cromwell Current, where the giant squid evading the stunning clicks of sperm whales has never yet been seen by man. Could I feel the clicks myself? I peered into the limpid darkness and thought I could see a muscular body glide past. Once more I felt like a spirit in another world. We turned around at 54 metres, but just then it might as well have been 1,000 metres. With regret I left the hunting whale, which I never saw. I will never know whether my enchantment was the result of my previous encounters or simply the first signs of nitrogen narcosis, 'raptures of the deep' as it is sometimes called. In Galapagos it is not always easy to know when one is dreaming.

The sun penetrates eerily into dream-like Galapagos seas, highlighting turtles and surgeonfish, Cape Douglas, Fernandina.

Wolf Island

Girdled by towering, guano-painted drop-offs (right), Wolf is a classic seabird island. Frigates and boobies by the thousands nest on the high, cactus covered plateaus (far right), masked boobies riding the sea winds to their nests (below), while tropic birds and swallow-tailed gulls seek the cliff faces. The most amazing bird, however, is Darwin's tiny sharp beaked ground finch, dubbed 'vampire finch' (centre, right), whose extraordinary habit in times of drought is to puncture the tail or wing feathers of nesting seabirds to drink their blood when food and moisture are scarce.

Darwin Island

Nearly unscalable cliffs make Darwin the ultimate outpost island, complete with its own microcosm of life, which it shares with Wolf, seemingly lost in mid-ocean. A small tuff stone arch just offshore attests to the relentless pounding of the seas (below) while the air above the island is alive with seabird traffic (near right), particularly at dusk and dawn. Tree-nesting red-footed boobies and their ground-nesting masked cousins apportion the available space amicably (centre right). For unknown reasons, a large proportion of red-foots here are white (far right), unlike the brown form more common elsewhere in Galapagos. Darwin is home to the only Galapagos colony of extremely graceful, tropically widespread sooty terns (far right, below).

The timeless tortoise world of Alcedo Volcano wakens to a cloud filled caldera.

10 AGONY AND REBIRTH IN TORTOISELAND
The Isabela Project

When I wrote about the giants of Alcedo Volcano ten years ago, I warned of the impending disaster looming over this timeless wonderland. Feral goats had invaded from the southern part of Isabela Island by crossing the bare lava fields of the Perry Isthmus, once thought impassable.

Five hundred thousand years ago similar giant tortoises ranged over the great plains of North America and other parts of the globe, leaving only their fossil remains to recount their tale of disappearance in the face of mammalian competitors and predators. Through human influence, they had now begun that same journey toward oblivion on Alcedo, but at a vastly accelerated pace. By the time the first edition of this book went to press, these were the words I chose to express the beginning of this agony:

'In the last couple of years, like an invading army, the goat population has suddenly mushroomed, laying bare the land under the gentle gaze of the ancient tortoises. As these words are being written the green tortoise meadows are turning to dust, the bush-clad caldera walls to eroding landslides, tree fern stands to bare stumps, and fog-drip trees on the caldera rim to toppled skeletons. Like refugees in their own land, growing numbers of tortoises are crowding under dwindling shade trees, and already increased numbers of bleached shells dot the caldera floor in what may be the early signs of starvation and death from overheating.'

I also described how an international campaign, launched as a bi-institutional project of the Galapagos National Park and Charles Darwin

Left and above: The same spot photographed in 1985 and ten years later shows the devastation wrought by goats. Tree ferns and other delicate plants were replaced by rough grasses, while erosion scoured the land.

Drawn to temporary rainwater in a landscape stripped of plants, on hot days tortoises risk dying from sun exposure if there is no shade nearby.

Foundation, was gathering momentum to fight back. But the task would be huge, both financially and logistically far greater than anything ever undertaken before in Galapagos, or for that matter, anywhere in the world. Whether this campaign would succeed was anybody's guess. The jury was still out, the final chapter yet to be written, as I expressed in these sad parting words; 'Alcedo's time capsule has burst, spelling uncertainty for the grazers of old, who knew not a competitor for millions of years. Like never before the future of the giant tortoise lies in the balance. If action can be taken within a very short time nothing will be lost, the vegetation will recover and the giant tortoises be none the worse for wear from a lean few years. We must hope that the tortoise photo collection in this book does not become the emblem of a lost era.'

The intervening decade has been a tense and challenging one. From the onset, Project Isabela had its target set on the complete removal

Tortoises wait listlessly under remnant shade trees even as the massive Isabela Project, the largest successful island restoration effort in the world, concludes its final offensive in 2005. Within months plantlife rebounded.

of large introduced mammals from all of northern Isabela. Budgeted at 8.5 million US dollars, it was funded primarily by the Global Environment Facility of the United Nations Development Program, with extensive additional support from a large range of other sources, from the Friends of Galapagos worldwide network to the government budget of the National Park.

Building an entirely new logistical structure from scratch just to get the project started, without the benefits of any precedent whatsoever in Galapagos history, was an enormous undertaking. Felipe Cruz, Technical Director of the Isabela Project during its entire field operations, is a native of Floreana Island, the smallest human community in Galapagos, and he did not underestimate the difficulties that would have to be surmounted to work in such a remote setting.

International expertise was sought from as far away as Australia and New Zealand, and years went into planning. There were fuelling and maintenance systems to develop, safety protocols to establish, firearms and munitions to import, people and dogs to train, supply lines to devise, and a thousand other aspects to consider and details to implement. Specially trained dogs were imported from New Zealand, then cross-bred locally and their offspring also trained to assist hunters to track and round up goats without chasing them further into the wilderness. Also from New Zealand, a helicopter company with vast experience in aerial hunting was selected, its highly skilled pilots being key during thousands of hours of precision flying and heart-stopping, near-ground manoeuvres.

Once the preparation phase of the project had been completed, the first field operation focused on Santiago Island as a practical training ground, being smaller and more accessible than Isabela. With new technology available for the first time, the project took over from 30 years of traditional ground hunting to root out the terribly destructive feral pigs. In 2002 Santiago was confirmed pig-free, followed by feral donkeys in 2004. At the same time nearly 60,000 goats had been reduced to scattered individuals being tracked down with the use of 'Judas goats' wearing radio collars that could easily be located as they joined wild ones. Immediately the vegetation started to rebound all over the island, with rare plants no longer confined to small protective enclosures and tree seedlings popping up everywhere across the deserted plains. While this dramatic turn-around came too late for the Santiago population of land iguanas, already extinct years ago, the secretive little endemic rails began to proliferate and the

Top and above: In a race against time the Isabela Project took shape during the 1990s, even as goat herds transformed the landscape from forest to dust.

Santiago giant tortoise could also start the slow process of rebuilding its depleted numbers.

Finally Project Isabela was ready to tackle its original goal and raise the world standards of ecological restoration to entirely new heights. But in the interim the tortoiseland of Alcedo, which had been so very dear to me — indeed where I'd set my life's course as a photographer — had started to look more and more like a wasteland. Courtesy of Project Isabela, I was able to document the changes to the tortoise habitat in 1995, 2000 and 2005, and each time I was barely able to recognize what I had known from my previous visit.

In 2000, of the dense, almost impenetrable thickets of endemic *Darwiniothamnus*, cats-claw and head-high bunchgrass, which had stood, once festooned in morning glories and delicate passion vines where mockingbirds frolicked, only bedraggled clumps remained. On the wetter southeasterly side of the volcano, the lush endemic *Scalesia* forest had been converted to an airy parkland, unpalatable grasses (to both goats and tortoises) having replaced the damp understorey of maidenhair ferns and rambling *Tournefortia* tangles. Giant tortoises crowding under their scant canopies for shade or moisture were hastening the trees' demise by rubbing away their bark and scraping bare their exposed roots. The verdant caldera floor meadows where tortoises used to graze and mate had been reduced to earthen pans, and herds of goats in their hundreds raised clouds of dust as they gambolled across the expanding plains.

When I revisited my old favourite areas again in 2005 the scene of devastation that awaited me nearly broke my heart. But at the same time a whole other story was also running its course, for Project Isabela had launched its final offensive on an unprecedented level of intensity and scale. A base station had been erected on the eastern shore of the volcano and temporary rain-catching shelters dotted at regular intervals all across its rugged southern flank. Foot teams and their trained dogs worked the ground while helicopter flights drew grid patterns across the map until no corner of this vast landscape had been left unchecked. Personnel and supplies were shuttled to the remotest spots and Judas goats released in key areas. Only a few months into the operation, success hung in the air like a fast-crystallizing mirage.

With the vegetation fast regenerating, a tortoise searches for edible plants among steaming fumaroles at sunrise.

To a long-lived tortoise the passage of goats was but a bad dream.

These are my impressions watching this extraordinary reversal of destiny and the startling vision of contrasts that I experienced that day:

'A huge, ancient tortoise — giant among giants — rests unmoving under a scraggly tree barely casting enough dappled shade to save it from the killer midday sun. This is a scene from Hell. Where the native *Scalesia* forest once stood, now only a handful of moribund trees dot a dusty, desert-like scene, each sheltering one or two more tired tortoises. Today a sere wind is blowing and, with roots no longer holding in the denuded ground, their remnant skeletons are toppling one by one as I watch.

'The old male tortoise slowly raises his head and sniffs the air, moist eyes scanning the desolate landscape before resuming his resigned siesta, chin on the ground. The skin around his neck is wrinkled and furrowed like an old crumpled newspaper, his fat reserves long spent, his armoured body deeply emaciated. He is waiting for deliverance, having endured in patient reptilian fashion the rampant goat invasion which has laid waste to his volcanic homeland over the past 20 years.

With renewed mating fervour an ancient tortoise mistakes a young male for a smaller female.

'Yet at the eleventh hour, his wait is fast drawing to an end. An incongruous sound is wafting on the wind: The whop-whop-whop of a helicopter, until this year never before heard on Alcedo. With the urgency of a bee making honey, the small chopper shuttles back and forth across the volcano, ferrying hunters and gear and running survey track lines.

'The imminent victory for conservation is literally throbbing in the air. Day by day, week by week, the goats that ran here in herds of thousands are vanishing — have vanished — and the transformation of the landscape is already in full swing. The ecological recovery is literally visible as an advancing green line. The contrast between raw devastation on one side of the caldera, the last goat stronghold, and the other, where regrowth has already begun, is nothing short of riveting.

'To the west, windswept plains and gaping ravines are dotted with bleached tortoise carapaces attesting to their inability to find shade while searching for scant plantlife to graze. The dense thickets are but a distant memory, the desolation made even more acute by recent drought.

'A half hour walk to the east and at once I feel as though I have stepped

forward through time. Here *Scalesia* seedlings are springing up beneath the few surviving old trees, with light rains having cast a vivid green flush on the land. Some saplings are already nearly one metre tall, having survived unscathed through the dry season for the first time in a decade. *Tournefortia* shrubs, stripped bare of leaves only a few months ago, have resprouted and are once again offering copious shade to contentedly sleeping tortoises. Darwin's finches sing from the foliage and already a few shy ferns are appearing in damp hollows. It is clear that it will not be long before the scars of a close call with an ecological holocaust will be naturally erased.

'For the first time in two decades I return from Alcedo feeling like I am walking on air, a sensation accentuated by flying rather than walking, for the very first time, to the caldera rim and back. Seeing is believing, yet it takes me a while to fully absorb the triumph before my eyes.'

In the final stages of Project Isabela, neither air accidents, funding shortages nor a myriad of other vicissitudes could hold the teams back, barely resting for weeks on end. In July 2006 the director of the Galapagos National Park announced that Project Isabela had achieved the impossible.

Not only Alcedo, but Darwin, Wolf and Ecuador Volcanoes and all of the previously untrodden lands in between as well, were finally declared goat free. Even on the two southern volcanoes of Sierra Negra and Cerro Azul which are much more difficult to tackle because of their size and ruggedness, goats have been reduced to such low numbers that the threat of future reinvasion can be safely contained.

A truly Herculean task whose outcome many had doubted, Project Isabela took almost ten years from concept to completion, during which time helicopters combed areas totalling more than the entire surface of the State of Rhode Island, and ground hunters walked distances equivalent to more than two thirds round the globe.

As I add the final words to their extraordinary story, the Alcedo giant tortoises are in the midst of a new rainy season, well-fed and demonstrating all of the breeding fervour I first witnessed in 1970. For me — and for the world — knowing that they will not join the ranks of dinosaurs after all is a dream come true, thanks to the vision of a few, and the support of thousands.

Stop Press! As I review the final proofs of this 10th year edition, I am once again in Galapagos and have just returned from a magical four-day re-immersion in tortoiseland. The hordes of goats have vanished, and where their thundering hooves once raised dust clouds, now armies of young waist-high *Scalesia* trees have sprung up around scraggly old survivors. Even though Alcedo is currently in the grips of another intense drought, morning glory vines are spreading like a vivid quilt, and the endemic daisy shrub *Darwiniothamnus* has been reborn from the pumice ground. Fog dripping from new ferns and *Lycopodium* clubmosses are dampening the parched earth. And everywhere tortoises are feeding contentedly on their favourite herbs, or sleeping under the spreading velvet leaves of *Tournefortia* shrubs. Their primal mating grunts fill the air in disregard for the drought. Amazingly, fresh new growth rings are appearing between their shell plates long worn smooth with age, even among those that appear fully mature. To these ancient beings the passage of the goats was but a bad dream.

Before the goats arrived, the seasonal cycles of the giant tortoise remained largely intact on Alcedo Volcano, Isabela.

EPILOGUE: GALAPAGOS IN THE 21st CENTURY
A Conservation Review

The State of Innocence. Why is Galapagos considered unique in the world? Why has it been called 'A natural laboratory of evolution'? Undeniably, the climatic and geographical settings have played a crucial role in giving the islands their unique biota. But of equal, or perhaps even greater, significance is the fact humans came on the scene here much, much later than to other major groups of warm oceanic islands anywhere in the world. Studies of sub-fossil bird bones found in island caves all over the South Pacific have shown a staggering wave of

An inquisitive juvenile red-footed booby lands on Mark's head, Genovesa.

extinction travelling from west to east across the ocean basin during the last few thousand years. This wave followed neatly in the wake of early Polynesian colonization, and numbered in the thousands of species. Amazingly, perhaps thanks to their location placing them at the end of this west-to-east migration pattern, the Galapagos were spared this human-induced mass extinction, the scale of which has not been rivalled since the demise of the dinosaurs.

Like on other oceanic islands, the entire evolutionary lineage of the Galapagos animals was moulded in the absence of large, efficient predators. As a result, fear as an instinctive reaction conveyed no practical benefit worthy of passing on through the generations, thereby nurturing a state of innocence among island species. When the first humans came ashore, birds sat on sailors' hats and tortoises and iguanas allowed themselves to be killed without any attempt to either flee or retaliate. This trust led to immediate abuse, as the hardy seafarers were not inclined to wax lyrical over virgin nature. A line from Captain David Porter, Commander of the US Navy frigate *Essex* in 1812, sums up these early encounters, 'we at first supposed they [marine iguanas] prepared to attack us. We soon, however, discovered them to be the most timid of animals, and in a few moments knocked down hundreds of them with our clubs.'

During a period that lasted about seventy years, from the 1790s to the 1860s, the Galapagos waters ran red with the blood of sperm whales, fuelling the demand for their oil on both sides of the Atlantic. When the supply dwindled around the turn of the century, the hapless giant tortoises briefly became the target of the oil commerce. Soon after this time a rampant world sealing industry in quest of pelts fell upon the Galapagos fur seals and very nearly drove them to extinction. Today, Galapagos wildlife continues to exhibit the same trusting nature it did centuries ago. In fact, with the flow of thousands of visitors whose behaviour and activities are closely controlled by National Park rules, the animals have become even more oblivious to human presence, a trait which imparts on the sensitive soul an almost magical attunement to nature.

The Alien Onslaught. By far the most insidious aspect of early human impact on the Galapagos fauna began with the release of a whole slew of foreign species — sometimes intentionally, sometimes not — long

The author's mother Jacqueline De Roy feeds scraps to appreciative pelicans and frigates, Academy Bay, Santa Cruz.

Feral donkeys trample tortoise nests, Isabela.

Feral dogs have decimated native species from reptiles to seabirds, Isabela.

before the first colonists started building their shacks on the lava shore. Goats were set free to provide meat for passing ships. Wild dogs soon joined them, purportedly released by the then Spanish Viceroy of Peru in an attempt to reduce the goats and thus hinder the buccaneers who plagued the Spanish trading fleets. Unintentional introductions took place when livestock set ashore temporarily to graze, such as pigs and cattle, were lost. The same happened with pack animals, like the horses and donkeys used to transport tortoises or tortoise oil, which made for the hills at the first opportunity. Finally, cats, rats and mice became established on many islands during shipwrecks, often surviving far more successfully than the human castaways.

The effect of this mammalian onslaught was intense and unrelenting. Cattle, goats and, to a lesser extent, horses were responsible for turning lush vegetation to open grasslands. Donkeys trampled tortoise nests. Pigs systematically dug up the eggs of giant tortoises and sea turtles, and ravaged Galapagos dark-rumped petrels and other ground nesting birds. Dogs preyed on anything from young tortoises, fur seals and sea lions to full-grown iguanas, penguins, flightless cormorants and many more native species. In some areas cats have been responsible for the complete breeding failure of land iguanas by eating all hatchlings, plus the disappearance of ground nesting birds like doves. Rats attacked hatchling tortoises and all manner of other small animals.

Sadly, the introduction of destructive species to Galapagos is not just a legacy from the past. Smooth-billed anis, the only introduced bird gone wild, were surreptitiously released as late as the 1970s in the erroneous belief that they would keep ticks off domestic cattle. For a while people's tame pigeons, notorious carriers of avian diseases, began nesting in natural areas near some villages until they were successfully eliminated just a few years ago.

Expanding agriculture has also allowed the escape of many plants and other organisms into the native habitat. For example, the last few decades have seen the dramatic transformation of vast areas of highland vegetation on Santa Cruz from ferns and *Miconia* shrubbery to a dense forest of introduced quinine trees, whose seeds are wind borne. On Floreana, San Cristobal and parts of Isabela, the problem is guayava and *Lantana* scrub. And in the last decade several particularly aggressive species of blackberry are spreading like wildfire as a result of recent covert introductions.

These are only a few examples of the enormous problems encountered when a delicate and isolated ecosystem is opened to the outside world.

The Flagship of Conservation. Efforts to preserve the Galapagos began as far back as the turn of the century, when various eminent scientific organizations and individuals expressed alarm at the impending annihilation of the unique Galapagos fauna and flora, as had already occurred in many other island groups. In 1935, exactly one hundred years after Charles Darwin's famous visit, the government of Ecuador enacted the first protective legislation, although this momentum was soon lost with the onset of World War II. On another centenary date, 1959, which commemorated the publication of Darwin's revolutionary book, *On the Origin of Species*, 98 per cent of the entire land area of the archipelago was declared Ecuador's first National Park. The only areas excluded from stringent protective legislation were those lands that had already been settled by a few hundred colonists. This event came with strong impetus from, and in tandem with, the creation of the international Charles Darwin Foundation for the Galapagos Isles (CDF), headquartered in Brussels. Under the auspices of the United Nations Educational, Scientific and Cultural Organization (UNESCO), the following year work began to construct the Charles Darwin Research Station (the CDF's operative arm) in Academy Bay, inaugurated in 1964. In 1968 the

Feral pigs on Santiago Island used to devastate ground nesting birds, sea turtles and giant tortoises. Ending a 30 year restoration campaign, they were eliminated in 2002 and goats three years later, allowing the ecosystem to recover at last.

Park wardens face the arduous task of monitoring native species . . .

. . . and controllong introduced ones.

Galapagos National Park Service also established its presence, and the two organizations have worked hand-in-hand ever since. Through a long-standing agreement signed with the government of Ecuador — a unique contract between a sovereign nation and an international non-government organization — the CDF was vested with the mandate to further scientific knowledge of the islands and provide advice and support to ensure their preservation.

For nearly half a century the Darwin Station and National Park have laboured assiduously together to secure the ecological integrity of the islands and to manage ever more complex pressures coming to bear from the outside. Together they have struggled against many odds, from ecological conundrums to political expedients, while facing the continual challenge of insufficient funding, the former depending on international charity, the latter on erratic government budgets.

In spite of these vicissitudes, enormous achievements have been attained, reversing the slide toward extinction of a number of endemic species, populations and races, while tackling the formidable challenge of eliminating introduced pest species, from insects to ungulates. As a result, one island after another, increasing in size as well as ecological and geographical complexity over the years, has seen its ecosystem restored to a pristine or near-pristine state. These extraordinary successes include:

- **Santa Fe:** Has its own endemic species of land iguana and rice-rat, plus several plant varieties, and is a stronghold for Galapagos hawks and doves; **goats** and **fire-ants** exterminated, no other introduced species known; vegetation recovered, no native species lost, **ecosystem restored**.
- **Española:** Home to the most extreme type of saddleback tortoise, largest lava lizard and most colourful subspecies of marine iguana, extraordinary land bird community including ground-foraging mockingbird (evolved in the absence of native rodents), nesting site for the entire world population of waved albatross,

plus largest colonies of several key seabirds (endemic swallow-tailed gulls and Nazca boobies, native red-billed tropicbirds and blue-footed boobies); **goats** exterminated, no other introduced species known; 40 years of saddleback tortoise captive breeding produced over 1000 reintroduced young from just 14 original adult survivors, now breeding again in the wild; vegetation recovering (giant cacti still scarce), no native species lost, **ecosystem restored**.

- **Marchena:** Endemic lava lizard and plant species; **goats** and **fire-ants** exterminated, no other introduced species known; vegetation recovered, no native species lost, **ecosystem restored**.
- **Pinta:** Endemic lava lizard and saddleback tortoise, down to one individual 'Lonesome George' awaiting fate in breeding centre; **goats** exterminated, no other introduced species known; vegetation recovered, one key native species lost, **ecosystem may be restored** in future by introducing similar tortoise type.
- **Santiago:** Endemic tortoise, rice-rat and plants; **pigs**, **goats** and **donkeys** exterminated after 30 year campaign, rats remain; flightless rail population and vegetation recovering rapidly, including critically endangered *Scalesia* species; rice-rat rediscovered after feared extinct, land iguana lost; **ecosystem partially restored**.
- **Isabela:** Five distinct giant tortoises, major nesting grounds for rare endemic penguins and flightless cormorants, critically endangered endemic mangrove finch; **goats** and **donkeys** exterminated from northern volcanoes in world's largest successful eradication campaign (see chapter on Project Isabela, page 148), **goats** and **dogs** reduced to non-viable remnants on southern volcanoes; **rats** and **cats** remain, plus **pigs** and **cattle** in south only; giant rat mysteriously extinct (known only from bones), no other species lost; **ecosystem partially restored**.
- **Pinzon:** Endemic saddleback tortoise and lava lizard; removal of wild tortoise eggs for captive raising and

After 40 years of captive breeding some of the young Española saddlebacks such as this one have matured and started reproducing in their original habitat.

In early 2000 the 1000th baby saddleback tortoise was released back on Española Island as part of the yearly batch of young hatched in captivity from a scant original 14 survivors.

release has boosted population unable to breed naturally due to rat predation, plus failed rat eradication attempt on foot provided several years' respite; current plans for aerial rat eradication in progress; no native species lost; **ecosystem to be restored**.

- **Fernandina, Genovesa, Darwin, Wolf:** Major strongholds of key endemics (e.g. fur seal, land iguana, marine iguana, hawk, penguin, flightless cormorant) and marine species including pelagic seabirds and fish; no species introduced except for transient anis during rainy season; no native species lost (except for mysterious natural disappearance of Fernandina tortoise, see page 127, last paragraph of chapter 8); legal protection and vigilance has sustained pristine state; **ecosystems intact**.

A Tourism Mecca. For many years it took a truly intrepid spirit to visit the Galapagos. There were basically two options. Either you set up your own expedition, as did such varied personalities as the American tycoon Allan Hancock on his private vessel *Velero III* in the 1930s and Prince Philip, Duke of Edinburgh, in the Royal Yacht *Britannia* in 1964. Or you sought passage on a small overloaded freighter from the port of Guayaquil, living among cattle, dried fish and indescribable heaps of cargo for a month as you journeyed into the unknown and back.

All that changed in 1969 when charter flights began bringing small groups of adventurous travellers regularly to the islands. Ships with modern amenities soon followed, allowing tourists to visit the islands in comfort and security. Fortunately, a symbiosis was established very early on between this budding industry, the Park administration and the Darwin Station. Between them, preliminary codes of conduct were drawn up, shipboard naturalists were trained and organized tourism began on an educational basis of the highest standard.

In the decades since then, tourism has expanded exponentially. Early on, dozens of local fishing boats converted to carrying passengers, and many dozens more were later built or imported to offer bigger and better amenities. Hotels too burgeoned, dotting the shoreline villages. Today a seemingly endless list of tour companies compete nationally and internationally to promote the perfect trip to Galapagos. Yet remarkably, with minor variations, the tour offerings still promote the same basic product: An opportunity, second to none in the world, to learn about, and commune with, nature.

Unlike Tahiti or Mallorca, this type of tourism offers a lifetime opportunity to open people's eyes and souls to the profound wonders of nature, to allow them to fall in love with its subtle harmony and to start caring, not just for Galapagos itself, but for the entire planet. Educating the world is what Galapagos tourism was born as — and should always remain focused on. Kept within these bounds, it is the only enterprise whose interests lie in an intact ecosystem, unlike alternative industries dependent upon natural resource extraction and consumption. As such, Galapagos tourism has every potential to remain the best argument in existence to counter a relentless barrage of other conflicting interests.

Fishing Controversy. It goes without saying that fishing is one of the oldest economic traditions in Galapagos, thanks to a combination of prolifically rich waters and no past history of over-exploitation. As a result, the marine ecosystem, like its terrestrial counterpart to which it is intimately bound, can boast a rare attribute on a global scale: To have made it through to the end of our second millennium largely intact.

Visitors from all walks of life flock to a wildlife experience unique in the world, Punta Suarez, Española.

Visitor numbers have increased by 14 per cent yearly, reaching 140,000 by 2006, with overcrowding becoming unsustainable.

The town of Puerto Ayora and its fishing fleet have grown exponentially in recent years.

Until the 1980s, Galapagos fishermen employed relatively simple fishing methods aimed at just three or four types of catch. Grouper was caught by hand-line, salted and dried, then shipped to the mainland prior to Easter as 'bacalao' for the traditional 'fanesca' served during Lent. Pelagic schools of large mullets, as well as the smaller coastal species, were also taken, using nets dragged by hand.

On the industrial scale foreign tuna purse-seining fleets (mostly Japanese and American) also worked Galapagos waters, but while their impact on dolphins and possibly other sea life must have been severe, this happened largely out of sight and out of mind, unchecked and unmonitored until Ecuador eventually succeeded in enforcing its 200 mile claim on territorial waters.

In the early sixties a small lobster enterprise began exporting frozen tails, which at first relied entirely on free-divers taking their catch by hand within breath-holding limits. Shallow diving depths and the lobsters' craggy hiding places served this budding industry as natural limiting factors. Later on, wet suits, air compressors, harpoons and night diving (when lobsters venture out to feed) vastly increased the divers' efficiency, bringing on the beginning of a lobster population decline.

Crucially, until the late 1980s only a few hundred resident fishermen at most were involved in Galapagos fishing. My father was one of them, partaking in both bacalao fishing and lobster diving in the 1950s and early 1960s.

But then something changed, not so much in the islands, but in the world. Global over-fishing was approaching catastrophic proportions from the Canadian Grand Banks to the Antarctic waters off South Georgia. The Peruvian coastal fisheries, with heavy involvement from Oriental fleets, collapsed. The effects of this crisis soon spilled over into

Ecuadorian waters. Suddenly, the near virgin state of the Galapagos marine environment became the irresistible focus of a seafood hungry world. Markets for shark fins and other goods never before considered by Galapagos fishermen were opened up, aided by shadowy transient middlemen. With the promise of vast profits, Galapagos fishers were encouraged by the foreign buyers to use new equipment and target different species, such as gillnetting sharks for their fins in total disregard for their protected status. The problem was compounded when larger vessels from Costa Rica, already heavily involved in the finning trade, began making regular poaching forays into Galapagos waters. Common by-products of this covert activity were drowned sea lions, penguins, marine iguanas and turtles, even though all are, of course, legally protected.

This was only the beginning of an era of major turmoil in Galapagos. Sea cucumbers, relished in Oriental cuisine, suddenly became another hot export commodity. Meanwhile fishing families along the coast of mainland Ecuador, confronted with dwindling returns in the face of resource depletion by foreign-backed industrial trawlers, scraped together the cost of passage to Galapagos. They arrived in ever increasing numbers, families and meagre belongings in tow, to make a new life on Isabela Island. Here the riches from the sea were only an arm's reach away.

The 1990s saw a gold-rush mentality take hold, while some parts of Galapagos became a kind of latter-day Klondike. Almost overnight, fleets of rapid speedboats equipped with surface-demand compressors began heading for the rich western waters of Galapagos, often under the cover of darkness. Crew members left tourism vessels to join in the craze. Large illicit camps sprang up hidden in the coastal mangrove forests of pristine Fernandina Island, where sea cucumbers in their millions were cured in mangrove-fuelled boilers. Boatloads of supplies arrived too, including live goats and chickens, and even prostitutes to entertain the fishermen. There were even unconfirmed reports of larger ships lurking offshore to transship the illicit product directly to international fleets, while

A dead white-tipped reef shark is but one of the discarded incidental kills, Academy Bay.

Poor habits from fishing and tourist boats alike are responsible for increasing shoreline refuse, Academy Bay.

hundreds of thousands of dollars were said to be moving through the local bank.

Politicians became involved, claiming their share, and some saw the fishing interests as their election ticket. As a result most management recommendations were sidelined. The authority of the National Park was challenged and for a while nullified by major audits, budget cuts and a string of politically appointed directors, none of whom lasted in the job for more than a few months. Attempts to curb the mayhem with sound scientific recommendations were met with threats and violence. The Isabela office of the National Park was gutted, and a park warden seriously injured by gunshot during a raid on a clandestine camp. Whenever catch quotas and seasons were set that did not entirely satisfy the fishing interests, gangs descended on both institutions and held them hostage until their demands were addressed.

During those sad days of madness, a cascade of other conservation problems ensued. The magnificent scallops, a rare endemic species, became a favourite ingredient in 'cebiche', a marinated seafood delicacy. Dried sea horses and black coral were commercialized as sidelines. Sea lion bulls were killed in response to Asian demand for their genitals. And the remains of over eighty slaughtered giant tortoises were discovered in the vicinity of fishing camps on Isabela, some consumed for food, others apparently killed as a message of defiance to the conservation world.

For nearly two decades the number of Galapagos fishermen skyrocketed, from 152 in 1982 to 392 in 1993, and finally peaked at 956 in 2002, with a total of 446 boats in operation. Efforts to check this rampant explosion were successfully thwarted through a combination of social and political fervour. Not surprisingly, within a few years the humble sea cucumber — an important organism which helps maintain the health of the marine ecosystem in a similar fashion as the earthworm does on land — had virtually been stripped from the coastal sea floor. Lobsters were fished with equal intensity.

With the main resources now severely depleted, attention turned to finding other alternatives. Long and protracted negotiations took place under huge pressure to open a new offshore longline fishery within the Galapagos Marine Reserve. After years of discussions and heated arguments, a major victory for conservation came when this notoriously destructive method was banned once and for all in all Galapagos waters. Finally, with the sobering lessons of the past, recent attention has shifted from unsustainable fishing practices to retraining opportunities and integration within the tourism industry.

A clandestine camp to process hundreds of thousands of sea cucumbers destroys mangroves and threatens pristine Fernandina with introduced species.

Modern Galapagos. Today it is a very different atmosphere that reigns in the once quiet fishing village of Puerto Ayora on whose outskirts I grew up, and where marine iguanas still tentatively bask on the busy town pier. Automobile traffic is now constant and disco music resonates from open-air bars. The man who now calls himself a Galapagos citizen is unlikely to have lived here more than a few years and is here not so much to admire the finches and tortoises, but more likely because Galapagos is Ecuador's fastest growing province. The true old-timer keeps him or herself mostly out of sight. As in many South American cities, crime and violence have arrived too, and civil unrest, as seen during the fishing debacle, has also become part of the Galapagos scene.

In 1998 a legal milestone of earth shattering proportions was achieved when the 'Special Law for Galapagos' was enacted, setting new development standards based on sustainable practices. This involves stringent immigration controls among other things, along with rulings on everything from the import of cars to pets and beverage containers. To enable this revolutionary legislation, and specifically to limit free movement of citizens between provinces, Ecuador first had to make a fundamental amendment to its constitution — the only country in

A ship rat escapes from the hold of the sinking freighter Iguana, *a constant threat to virgin islands, Academy Bay, Santa Cruz.*

the world to alter the constitutional rights of its citizenry for the sake of conservation. But the application of this visionary law has been slow and tortuous. In the last 30 years since tourism became a driving economic force in Galapagos, the resident population has been growing by six per cent annually, with the last available count from 2001 showing 18,640 inhabitants and rising fast. Almost two thirds live on Santa Cruz Island, which barely 800 souls called home during my childhood.

Ironically, one aspect that has not grown apace with other developments in the islands is the education system, with a complete overhaul and reform long-awaited but still no closer to being delivered. As a sad consequence, children educated in Galapagos schools find themselves ill-equipped to compete in the world at large. And when they leave to pursue higher education elsewhere, as many do, they frequently fail to meet entry-level requirements. This handicap, along with higher economic standards in Galapagos than on the mainland, skewed by the injection of tourist dollars, means that young Galapagueños have nowhere to turn to when seeking a life of their own. Hence, mushrooming population numbers coupled with limited opportunity is a time-bomb which needs addressing urgently.

Tourism is the only Galapagos industry that, in nearly four decades since its inception, has flourished unwaveringly. However, it too has followed an ever steepening growth curve in recent years, growing by seven to eight per cent annually and outpacing even the vertiginous population trends. By the end of 2006 Galapagos received some 145,000 annual visitors. Consequently, air traffic has also skyrocketed by 10 per cent a year, with up to six or eight commercial flights landing on a single day, most operating at full capacity. As a result, where the visitor once stepped ashore on beaches so pristine it felt like he or she was the first person to arrive since Charles Darwin had sailed away, now groups are likely to have to queue up for access to the best views. Fortunately, the focus of the industry (as mentioned earlier) has wavered little from

162

a conservation-oriented educational experience. The real danger will come should hotels begin to expand into resorts, and activities such as sports fishing, sometimes touted as a valid form of 'diversification', were to shift the emphasis away from the look-but-don't-touch approach.

Happily, the impact of those ever-increasing numbers has thus far not noticeably stressed any part of the wild ecosystem, thanks to the maintenance of that simple motto first applied by the Sierra Club groups in the late sixties: 'Take only photos, leave only footprints.'

Yet those footprints are becoming undeniably larger and deeper, and the collateral effects profound and insidious. Not only is tourism largely responsible for fuelling the demographic explosion in Galapagos, it has also caused — and continues to cause on an accelerating scale — a cascade of stresses and threats, both real and potential. These range from the booming local economy placing higher and higher demands on natural resources, e.g. construction materials (rocks, sand, wood), seafood (fish, molluscs, octopus), water (more and more ambitious drilling projects), sanitation (septic tanks, landfills), to direct impact of the tour vessels themselves, including fuel consumption, garbage disposal and raw sewage discharge at sea.

The Alien Threat Returns. With every cargo ship delivering goods to the residents and tourism operations alike, with each delivery of fuel for tour ships or town generators, and with escalating numbers of daily flights carrying fresh goods and passengers alike, the threat of a biological holocaust comes one step nearer. Twice already there have been close calls with substantial oil spills, both diesel and bunker fuel, leaking into the sea when a cargo ship (MV *Iguana*) and tanker (MV *Jessica*) ran aground on their approaches into Galapagos harbours. Luckily, in neither case were the effects disastrous at

Barge loads of cargo are brought ashore from the Guayaquil freighter, responsible for recent insect introductions.

A mushrooming resident population coupled with a fast-growing economy are stressing the natural resources such as this gravel quarry on Santa Cruz Island, burrowing deep into what was once an extinct volcanic scoria cone.

ecosystem level, but next time things could be very different depending on circumstance and location.

Yet the truly chilling threat to Galapagos probably lies not in petrochemicals or other pollutants, but in the risks of invasion by new biological agents and pathogens. Even with the major successes in reversing the legacy of past introduced species, new ones are still establishing beachheads and taking advantage of the fact that modern Galapagos has lost its most formidable defence ever: Geographical isolation.

With the frenetic expansion of human activity this natural ecological barrier, so effective for millions of years, has crumbled. Already a new slew of introduced plants and insects, along with alien geckoes and frogs (the first amphibians in Galapagos) have gained major toeholds in recent years. On San Cristobal Island a ravenous blackfly has chased farmers from their lands around the only freshwater stream in Galapagos, so unbearable is its bite. A newly introduced botfly is attacking and killing finch chicks in their nest, while avian pox severely affects fledglings.

Still this is nothing compared to what is yet to come if this terrible biosecurity breach is not urgently resealed. Canine distemper recently swept through the local pet dog population, with the potential of jumping species and devastating the endemic fur seal and sea lion colonies. The dreaded West Nile virus has reached South America, its nefarious effects recently reported from as close as Colombia. The mosquito vector for this lethal bird pathogen, known to have ravaged captive penguins and other seabirds when it infested zoo populations in North America, is one of the introduced species already well established in Galapagos. So is the carrier of avian malaria, responsible for driving many species of Hawaiian honeycreepers — the evolutionary equivalents of Darwin's finches — to extinction.

163

The 1998 Special Law for Galapagos prescribed a strict quarantine regime for all goods and crafts bound for the islands. Accordingly, an ambitious inspection program, relying on X-ray machines, sniffer dogs and human inspectors, is charged with screening all luggage, cargo and merchandise. Yet the continuous flow by air and sea, including rising numbers of private jets, far outstrips the system's ability to cope. Bug-proof hangars and round-the-clock surveillance will be needed in all departure and arrival ports before the net can be tightened sufficiently to avert a future disaster which, quite possibly, lurks literally around the corner.

Where to from here? Strangely perhaps, there is a tendency the world over for organizations and individuals alike to think of Galapagos conservation as such a worthy cause that, surely, its technical and financial needs have long since been secured. So much so that it may come as a surprise that such fundamental items as the salary of the Darwin Station Director, or spare parts for the Park's patrol boats, cannot be ensured from one month to the next. Little wonder, then, that time and again vital conservation work has been delayed and interrupted by necessity.

The vast majority of visitors to Galapagos are so moved by their immersion into this peaceful natural world that they would genuinely do anything to ensure its survival. With the future of Galapagos in the balance like never before, tour companies are at last preparing to take ownership of the problems which traditionally were left to conservation managers to sort out. On-board fundraising programs have proven highly successful, and new ideas are being floated for private businesses to pitch in much more proactively than in the past. It is in everyone's best interest that these collaborative pathways be explored fully — and fast.

Commercial buildings, tarmac and heavy traffic in Puerto Ayora have replaced many of the sandy pathways and small lava-rock houses of my childhood.

Through these days of tumult and change, a new awareness of the problems and solutions is emerging among young island citizens.

Visitors frequently ask me what they can do to ensure the safe future of Galapagos. The first thing, whether before you book a trip or even after you return, is to ask of your tour company what their active role has been. Have they ever provided equipment or transport to scientists or Park personnel in the field? Have they ever made a donation to Galapagos conservation or urged their passengers to do so? Do they look carefully at the source of food, such as fish or lobster, served aboard the ships they use? If they do not believe in actively nurturing the resource upon which their business relies, let them know you will shop elsewhere — there are literally dozens of choices despite some company slogans proclaiming otherwise.

Write letters of support to the Galapagos National Park and Charles Darwin Research Station expressing your appreciation for what they and the government of Ecuador have done so far, and why you feel it is important to continue doing so. Such letters can serve as vital ammunition against insidious political attack.

Please remember, too, that nothing will ever serve the cause better than simple funding, no matter what size the donation. Fifty dollars will buy a pair of boots for a Park warden, five hundred may support a patrol boat operation, and five thousand could be enough to carry out an annual census of threatened birds such as the flightless cormorant or mangrove finch.

The difference between Galapagos conservation and similar work elsewhere in the world is that here the battle can still be won with relative ease. Galapagos biodiversity is still virtually intact, with almost no species lost to date. The island ecosystem, while stressed and threatened in identifiable areas, is by no means broken. In Galapagos the choice of whether to lose it or save it is a luxury upon which we still have the opportunity to act freely. Should we someday discover that we've let that opportunity pass, then where else in the world would there be any hope left?

A PERSONAL PLEA

If your own impression of Galapagos, whether by visiting or through reading this book, has moved you to want to become personally involved in their fate, then please think about your next step.

These wondrous islands CAN be saved and each one of us CAN become part of that success story for posterity. The tools are in place with know-how built up over 50 years, but what is still needed is the fuel — the financial security to execute conservation strategies and visions with long-term confidence.

If you have read the Epilogue herewith, and would like to make a real and lasting difference, please contact one of the following organizations nearest you:

Galapagos Conservancy
(formerly Charles Darwin Foundation, Inc.)
Contact: Johannah Barry
407 North Washington Street,
Suite 105 Falls Church, VA 22046, USA
Tel: +1 703 538 6833
Email: darwin@galapagos.org
Website: www.galapagos.org

Charles Darwin Foundation of Canada
Contact: Garrett Herman
55 Avenue Road, Suite 2250, Toronto,
ON M5L 3L2, Canada
Tel: +1 416 964 4400
Email: garrett@lomltd.com

Galapagos Conservation Trust
Contact: John Harris
5 Derby Street, London W1J 7AB, United Kingdom
Tel: +44 (0) 20 7629 5049
Fax: +44 (0) 20 7629 4149
Email: gct@gct.org
Website: www.gct.org

Friends of Galapagos New Zealand
Contact: Julian Fitter
PO Box 11-639, Wellington, New Zealand
Tel/Fax. +64 (0) 4 476 3241
Mobile +64 (0) 4 476 3241
Email: info@galapagos.org.nz
Website: www.galapagos.org.nz

The Japan Association for Galapagos (JAGA)
C/o Nature's Planet, 3-15-13-403 Kita-Aoyama,
Minato-ku, Tokyo 107-0061, Japan
Tel/Fax +81 (0) 3 5766 4060
Email: info@j-galapagos.org
Website: www.j-galapagos.org

Zoologische Gesellschaft Frankfurt
Contact: Christof Schenk
Alfred-Brehm-Platz 16 60316, Frankfurt, Germany
Tel: +49 (0) 69 943 4460
Email: info@zgf.de
Website: www.zgf.de

Freunde der Galapagos Inseln
Contact: Claudia Poznik
c/o Zoo Zurich Zurichbergstr,
221 8044 Zurich, Switzerland
Tel: +41 (0) 1 254 2670
Email: galapagos@zoo.ch
Website: www.galapagos-ch.org

Nordic Friends of Galapagos
Contact: Kenneth Kumenius
Korkeasaari 00570, Helsinki, Finland
Tel: +358 50 564 4279
Email: k.kumenius@kolumbus.fi
Website: www.galapagosnordic.fi

Stichting Vrienden van de Galapagos Eilanden
Contact: Ans D. Thurkow-Hartmans
Binnenweg 44 6955, AZ Ellecom, The Netherlands
Tel/Fax: +31 313 421 940
Email: fin.galapagos@planet.nl
Website: www.galapagos.nl

The Galapagos Darwin Trust
Banque Internationale à Luxembourg 2,
Boulevard Royal L-2953, Luxembourg
Donations marked 'For the Galapagos' may be made
to Account No.1-100/9071
Email: cdrs@fcdarwin.org.ecg

A MESSAGE FROM
Dr. Graham Watkins,
Executive Director
Charles Darwin Foundation
Isla Santa Cruz, Galapagos, Ecuador
Mail: Casilla 17-1-3891, Quito,
Ecuador
Email: cdrs@fcdarwin.org.ecg
Website: www.darwinfoundation.org

Since the Charles Darwin Foundation was established nearly five decades ago almost everything in Galapagos has changed. With 48 years behind us as the organization dedicated exclusively to the permanent preservation of the Galapagos natural heritage, we have much to celebrate, having helped these islands become a world conservation icon. In preparation for our milestone 50th anniversary, the CDF has reorganized and revitalized itself and is poised to lead the renaissance of Galapagos through the next half century. Some of our future objectives include: Becoming the world centre for island sustainability research and developing a Darwin-based visitor experience second to none, undertaking a world class process of educational reform, building a world class international vocational training institute in Santa Cruz, implementing a model school in Isabela, getting rid of goats from all of Galapagos, eradicating rats from all the smaller islands, rehabilitating completely Floreana Island including bringing back its critically endangered mockingbird, putting tortoises back on Pinta, protecting completely Darwin and Wolf Islands and their surrounding waters, and many more. If enough support from the international community is mustered, this vision of the CDF can be achieved, serving as a catalyst effect toward resolving the more complex governance issues of Galapagos. We invite you, the reader, to become an active part of this project.

International
League of
Conservation
Photographers

This book is endorsed by the International League of Conservation Photographers (ILCP), an initiative of the WILD Foundation, as a contribution toward the preservation of one of the world's most iconic conservation treasures.

Photographic Notes

For those interested in the technicalities, an outline of my equipment of choice follows. Although the majority of the photos on these pages were taken within the last six to eight years, some range back right through to the early 1970s and even before. Originally the only film type I used was Kodachrome II, with a pathetically slow rating of 25 ASA, though in those days I never used a tripod. Later I welcomed the arrival of Kodachrome 64, although this film was hopelessly sensitive to heat, producing many instances of horrible colour shifts. Nonetheless, I used this true and durable film until the early 1990s when Kodak stopped doing their own processing in the US (where all my film had to be shipped) and the quality of processing declined dramatically. After trying several new film types, I settled happily on Fuji Provia 100, with limited use of Velvia 50 on dull days when colours need reviving.

Likewise, my cameras and lenses have evolved over the years. The camera used to produce my very first published photos came to me by amazing circumstances. A visiting film-maker, Jack Couffer, working on a Walt Disney production, had decided the time had come for him to change cameras. When learning of my interest he bestowed upon me his rugged Pentax SLR and a short telephoto lens, in perfect working order. Although without a built-in light meter, it produced excellent results. I added various other lenses and eventually replaced it with a Spotmatic, fully-metered model, spending many years juggling awkward screw mount lenses on this virtually indestructible camera with ease. When the time came to look at the new bayonet mounts I opted for the ultra lightweight Olympus system, although I was disappointed to find that my quality had dropped. Eventually I switched to Nikon, going through various lightweight models and adding motor drive and more varied lenses.

For years I resisted heavy or complicated equipment that would slow down or otherwise impede my mobility, an approach that was ideal for the Galapagos environment. I never used a tripod and all of my gear, including film, fitted into a compact, home-made, plywood, watertight case (weighing just over seven kilograms) which rarely left my shoulder, even when having to swim ashore. Underwater photography was, and still is, carried out with a Nikon FE2 camera within an Ikelite housing or, more often, a simple Nikonos V, using Kodachrome 200 in most cases, or Provia 100 pushed one f-stop.

Today, like most photographers, I have modernized my equipment again by switching to the Nikon N90 and F5 models allowing for auto focus, auto exposure and, most importantly, delicately compensated fill flash. At last, though I still curse that added weight, a Benbo tripod, with Arca Swiss monoball head, has now become my trusted ally. Two camera bodies and a range of four lenses (18mm, 28–70mm, 80–200mm and a 300mm telephoto), travel with me everywhere, along with an SB25 flash and Quantum battery pack, all carried within an All Weather Lowepro case which so far has done sterling service in wave wash and tropical rain alike. A few more specialized items and lenses are also sometimes used, but not routinely carried. Filters play a very small part in my photography; only occasionally do I apply a polarizer on a wide-angle lens to increase perception in water and, even more infrequently, a split-neutral density filter to tone down a bright sky and thus minimize contrast with the subject.

All of the above film types and equipment models are represented within these pages.

Index